CW01376659

PROCLAIMING THE GOSPEL IN A SECULAR AGE

Proclaiming the Gospel in a Secular Age explores how a religion, Christian or any other focussing on a personal God, may be communicated to people in a secular age. With people uninterested, uninformed or unbelieving in the Godward dimension and in any particular religious tradition, David Attfield claims that appropriate communication is essential. Before direct communication can begin some background conditions in the targeted population must be satisfied, and communication then requires a series of stages.

This book offers an indepth examination of seven particular species for communication: evangelism; inter-faith dialogue; nurture of adults; nurture of children; religious education in schools; the academic study of religion; professional ministerial formation. Each form of communication is defined, theories applied, and the training of communicators outlined. David Attfield offers fresh insights and practical suggestions which will be of interest to a wide-range of students, academics and those in ministerial training and practice, with an interest in pastoral theology and religious education.

David G. Attfield is a retired Anglican priest and tutor at College of St Hilde & St Bede, Durham, UK. He has published extensively on religious education.

Ashgate New Critical Thinking in Theology & Biblical Studies

Ashgate New Critical Thinking in Theology & Biblical Studies presents an open-ended series of quality research drawn from an international field of scholarship. The series aims to bring monograph publishing back into focus for authors, the international library market, and student, academic and research readers. Headed by an international editorial advisory board of acclaimed scholars, this series presents cutting-edge research from established as well as exciting new authors in the field. With specialist focus, yet clear contextual presentation, books in the series aim to take theological and biblical research into new directions opening the field to new critical debate within the traditions, into areas of related study, and into important topics for contemporary society.

Series Editorial Board

Revd Dr Paul Fiddes, Regent's Park College, University of Oxford, UK
Revd Professor Jeffrey Astley, University of Durham and North of England Institute for Christian Education, UK
Professor Canon Anthony Thiselton, University of Nottingham, UK
Professor Timothy Jervis Gorringe, University of Exeter, UK
Professor Alan Torrance, St Andrews University, UK
Revd Professor Adrian Thatcher, College of St Mark & St John, Plymouth, UK
Professor Mary Grey, Sarum College, Southampton University, and University of Wales, Lampeter, UK
Professor Rebecca S. Chopp, Emory University, USA
Professor Judith M. Lieu, King's College London, UK
Professor Vincent Brummer, University of Utrecht, The Netherlands
Professor Gerhard Sauter, University of Bonn, Germany
Professor Terrence Tilley, University of Dayton, Ohio, USA
Professor Stanley J. Grenz, Carey Theological College, Vancouver, Canada
Professor Edward Farley, Vanderbilt University, USA
Professor Miroslav Volf, Yale University Divinity School, USA
Professor Richard Roberts, University of Lancaster, UK

Proclaiming the Gospel in a Secular Age
A general theory of religious communication

David G. Attfield

Ashgate
Aldershot • Burlington USA • Singapore • Sydney

© David G. Attfield 2001

All rights reserved. No part of this publication may be reproduced, stored in a retrieval system, or transmitted in any form or by any means, electronic, mechanical, photocopying, recording or otherwise without the prior permission of the publisher.

Published by
Ashgate Publishing Limited
Gower House
Croft Road
Aldershot
Hants GU11 3HR
England

Ashgate Publishing Company
131 Main Street
Burlington, VT 05401-5600 USA

Ashgate website: http://www.ashgate.com

British Library Cataloguing in Publication Data
Attfield, D. G. (David George), 1931-
  Proclaiming the gospel in a secular age : a general theory of
  religious communication. - (Ashgate new critical
  thinking in theology & biblical studies)
  1. Communication - Religious aspects - Christianity
  I. Title
  261.5'2

Library of Congress Cataloging-in-Publication Data
Attfield, David G.
    Proclaiming the Gospel in a secular age : a general theory of religious
    communication / David G. Attfield.
        p.   cm. -- (Ashgate new critical thinking in theology & biblical studies)
    Includes bibliographical references (p.) and index.
    1. Communication--Religious aspects--Christianity. I. Title. II. Series.
    BV4319.A88 2001
    230'.01'4--dc21   00-054277

ISBN 0 7546 1484 0

Printed and bound by Athenaeum Press, Ltd.,
Gateshead, Tyne & Wear.

Contents

1	Introduction		1
	(i) Autobiographical		1
	(ii) Defining the Key Terms		2
	(iii) Species of Communication		4
	(iv) Assumptions of the Theory		9
2	Current Forms of Religious Communication and their Problems		15
	(i) Church Decline and its Causes		15
	(ii) The Normal Process of Communication		17
	(iii) A Special Process of Communication		19
	(iv) Gender and Communication		21
	(v) A New Positive Approach		22
	(vi) The Requirements of Communication		24
3	The Core Theory		27
	(i) The Four-Stage Model		27
	(ii) Adding the Fifth Stage		28
	(iii) The Background Conditions		31
	(iv) The Second, the Communicator's Model		33
4	Background Conditions		37
	(i) Verbal Ability		37
	(ii) Autonomy		40
	(iii) Opportunity		43
5	Nourishing the Sense of God		47
	(i) The Sense of God		47
	(ii) Nourishing the Sense of God		49
	(iii) Assessing Stage IV		54
	(iv) The Case for God's Reality		55
6	Motivation and Myers-Briggs		61
	(i) The Myers-Briggs Typology		61
	(ii) Motivation by Type and Temperament		64
	(iii) Applying Myers-Briggs in Communication		67
	(iv) Other Categorisations		69
7	Learning, Exploration and Commitment		73
	(i) Learning		73
	(ii) Exploration		76
	(iii) Religious Truth-Criteria		79
	(iv) Reformed Epistemology		85
	(v) The Stage of Commitment		90

8	Application		97
	(i)	Evangelism	97
	(ii)	Inter-Faith Dialogue	99
	(iii)	Nurture of Adults	102
	(iv)	Child Nurture	104
	(v)	Religious Education	105
	(vi)	Academic Study of Religion	107
	(vii)	Ministerial Formation	109
9	Objections		117
	(i)	The Social Gospel	117
	(ii)	Grace and Human Effort	118
	(iii)	Lack of Resources	120
	(iv)	Remediation	123
10	Training the Communicators		127
	(i)	Who are the Communicators?	127
	(ii)	Evangelism	128
	(iii)	Inter-Faith Dialogue	132
	(iv)	Nurture of Adults	134
	(v)	Child Nurture	135
	(vi)	Religious Education	138
	(vii)	The Academic Study of Religion	141
	(viii)	Ministerial Formation	144
11	A Concluding Vision		149
	(i)	Summary of the Whole Argument	149
	(ii)	The Sower and the Seed	150
	(iii)	A Final View	154

Bibliography 157
Index 163

To my wife, Janet, without whose help and patience this book could not have been written.

I also want to express my gratitude to the Rev. Professor Jeff Astley for help and encouragement in the writing of this book.

Chapter 1

Introduction

Christians desire to communicate their faith and some followers of other religions seek to do the same. In this introduction I tell how my theory of religious communication has evolved; I define the key terms and clarify the concepts the theory requires; and I outline the assumptions on which my argument is conducted.

(i) Autobiographical

Soon after Ordination into the Ministry of the Church of England I learned how difficult it is to communicate the faith. I became a Lecturer in a Church College of Education, because I believed Christianity could be communicated by Religious Education in schools – as was still assumed in the early 'sixties – and that by sharing in the training of teachers I could indirectly contribute to this enterprise of passing on the faith on a wider scale than by being a parish-priest or teacher myself.

Later I became involved in teaching philosophy of education and the principles of Religious Education. In the light of developments in thought in the 'sixties, I came to realise that, although imparting religion could not be the proper purpose of multi-faith, open-ended Religious Education, yet much of what we envisaged in the motivation of pupils, their learning and their exploration, had something in common with any rational approach to evangelism and nurture. True, commitment could not now be professionally intended by the Religious Education teacher, but as an incidental result of the process, the adoption of faith could still be privately hoped and prayed for.

In the course of my reflection on Religious Education and the nature of the Christian nurture of children within the household of faith, I worked out an analysis of the processes involved. Pupils must be motivated to learn; contexts and programmes of learning have to be set up; students need encouraging to explore what they have learnt; and lastly the possibility of commitment should be held open and, within some enterprises, should be encouraged, if young people wish to proceed to this.

The latter part of my career was as a priest in urban working-class parishes. For years I was baffled by the sheer difficulty of communicating religion to people there, whether without or within the churches. The basic problem is complete lack of interest in what we have to offer. I felt I was like a salesman trying to sell a product noone wants to buy. Reflection led me to see that it is necessary to nurture people's sense of God before there can be any possibility of motivating them to learn about faith.

Further I realised that several background conditions of successful communication had to be satisfied before even this nurture could be attempted. A certain ability to use words was needed for people to be able to comprehend and to explore the Gospel. A measure of autonomy was also necessary since, in today's world, faith must be a matter of individual choice. And finally persons require an opportunity to learn, with sufficient leisure, free from the pressures of life, for them to be able to give the time, thought and attention that communication demands of the hearer.

For some years I had been interested in stage-theories in psychology: Piaget on intellectual development; Kohlberg on moral; and Erikson on social and personal. Fowler on faith-development particularly attracted me. Now I realised that, if I added my earlier idea of developing a sense of God to my analysis in terms of motivation, learning, exploration and commitment; and if I placed, prior to these tasks being successfully carried out, the need to satisfy the background conditions of verbal ability, autonomy and opportunity, then I had the makings of a stage theory of religious communication. It would be general enough to underpin all the main species of this genus, and broad enough to compass communication in other theistic faiths. So now I come in this book to present systematically my general Theory of Religious Communication, in a work which sums up and draws together thinking from the dominant concerns of my working-life.[1]

(ii) Defining the Key Terms

Before we can proceed to formulate our Stage Theory of Religious Communication, it is necessary to clarify and distinguish the activities to which, we claim, the Theory will apply in whole or in part. These enterprises are the Species of the Genus of Religious Communication: *Evangelism; Inter-Faith Dialogue; Nurture; Child-Nurture; Religious Education; the Academic Study of Religion* and *Ministerial Formation.*

Further in distinguishing these from one another, we need an adequate definition of a Christian. This and other definitions are intended as the minimum required to identify the class of person or activity in question. An adequate conception or characterisation of what may be essential to them or important to them is left an open issue in each case. For instance, a theologically richer account of what it is to be a Christian may be needed for many purposes other than those we have in mind.

Our definition of a Christian roughly reflects ordinary usage and covers the people we would normally want to call Christians, as opposed to those we would not. The definition to be given does indeed depart radically from the popular use of the term to mean a merely decent person, since this usage is incoherent. For what about the decent Jew, Muslim etc.? Any useful analysis of what a Christian is must surely be able to distinguish a follower of the Christian faith from adherents of other great religions, who may be equally morally worthy!

We suggest a Christian is a member of a mainstream church, by whatever are its own criteria of membership, and who has not repudiated his or her membership. Clearly if people claim to have become atheists or whatever and if they affirm that they are no longer Christians, they must be allowed to be so no more, despite perhaps membership of the church through Infant Baptism. Further we consider it better to define the term 'Christian' in terms of belonging to a religious community rather than in terms of belief or experience, since these today vary so widely among those one would normally want to call Christians. This definition through church membership has the substantial advantage of identifying Christians by their association with a well-marked, recognisable society in the real world.

Again by inserting into the definition 'mainstream', membership of marginal cults or sects is excluded and a workable criterion can be provided by further regarding 'mainstream' as a body belonging to the World Council of Churches or Churches Together in England or similar organisations in other countries. We are willing to accept that by our definition such thinkers as Simone Weil will not count as a Christian because she chose not to be baptised into the Roman Catholic church:[2] her status as a great spiritual writer may be recognised by calling her a near- or quasi-Christian or a Seeker after Christian truth.

Among Christians so defined, 'practising' Christians must be further distinguished from 'non-practising', in a way comparable to the use of such distinctions in respect to other faiths. Practice here means attendance at public worship. Within the class of the non-practising we also mark off 'lapsed' from what may be termed 'aborted' Christians. Lapsed are those who once practised but no longer do. The aborted are those who never began to practise, as with babies whose parents never again bring them to church once they have been baptised.

Within the class of practising Christians we also divide the 'committed' from the 'non-committed'. A committed Christian we define as one who not only practises his or her faith by attending public worship but who also has a degree of self-conscious religious identity in terms of belief and what he or she is bound to do to express that belief. With churches that practise pedo-baptism commitment may be roughly equated with being confirmed, though not exclusively so. (For commitment presupposes a minimal measure of knowledge and thought about one's own faith and in the past confirmation has been for some a nominal or merely formal affair.) It also follows that a young child cannot be a committed Christian, since some degree of maturity and understanding is necessary to being committed. In Fowler's terms at least his third Stage of Synthetic Conventional faith is required for it to be sensible to describe a person as a committed Christian.[3] This is the Stage when knowledge about Christianity is combined with a tendency to Christian practice (Synthetic), but faith is simply taken without choice or reflection from the Church in which the young person has been brought up (Conventional). Even with older children premature commitment, while in the throes of adolescence, is not to be encouraged any more than it is in other spheres like vocation or marriage. The commitment of faith is an adult affair at an age when some maturity has been attained.

(iii) Species of Communication

Now we can move on to using these definitions to distinguish from each other the activities our Theory covers when concerned with Christian Communication. With other theistic faiths, their adherents would have to elaborate parallel definitions to correspond with ours to cover the communicative enterprises they practise and to distinguish them from one another. The activities to be discussed may all be regarded as Species of Religious Communication: and for our purposes Communication is to be understood as the process whereby one person, the Communicator, conveys a message or skill, attitude or value, which he or she possesses already, to another person, whom we shall call from now on, the Communicatee (a term of art we have modelled on promisee or mortgagee, to denote the recipient of Communication); and this process must proceed in some intelligible way. (The last proviso is inserted to rule out coincidences, where there is no conceivable connection between the parties, having to be regarded as Communication.)

We distinguish seven Species within the genus of Religious Communication. They are: *Evangelism, Inter-Faith Dialogue, Nurture, Child Nurture, Religious Education, the Academic Study of Religion* and *Ministerial Formation*. These Species of Communication are different from each other in terms of the Communicator's *intention*. Human activities, as opposed to mere physical processes and random movements of our bodies, gain their character from what the agent intends, and his or her intention is often specified in the end-state, result or outcome they want to bring about. There are indeed puzzling cases where the actual outcome diverges from the intended outcome and the status of such activities may not be easy to characterise accurately. Such problems will be discussed after our seven Species have been considered one by one.

To begin with *Evangelism*. This we define as those communicative activities intended to cause a person to become a committed Christian for the first time, (and also those who have earlier lapsed from this category). For no evangelist would be content with causing anyone to become just a practising Christian without commitment. It is also important to notice that our definition is not in terms of describing the many and varied activities concerned, all of which may count as evangelism. Rather we work with the intention of causing someone to become a committed Christian,[4] provided that the Communicators are themselves practising or committed Christians, (or followers of another faith with their *Evangelism*.)

One further implication of this definition should be noted. It is indeed possible to evangelise children but because commitment belongs to adulthood and maturity, child evangelism is an enterprise that cannot by definition be properly completed in childhood.[5]

The next Species we shall discuss is *Inter-Faith Dialogue*. Some people may consider this another variation on *Evangelism*. But when the Communicatee already has a rich and complex religious or other ideological commitment, communicating religion to him or her has to have a special character and cannot be treated as *Evangelism*. The intention to convert and to produce a committed person has to be abandoned, since if it became obvious that such was the Communicator's intent, the Communicatee would be frightened off and would withdraw from serious conversation. Further the poor record of almost negligible Christian success in converting followers of other great faiths suggests that this evangelistic aim is not worth pursuing.

Commitment may, of course, be an incidental and unintended result of *Dialogue*: and that is why this Species of Communication could be regarded misleadingly as a variant on *Evangelism,* given our definition of *Evangelism* in terms of intended results. But the proper object and product of *Inter-Faith Dialogue* is *mutual* understanding and exploration. The earlier stages of the theory we shall outline can all be accommodated in *Dialogue*: however, the only commitment likely to be reached by the dialogist is to further dialogue and not to a change of faith-commitment in either of them. And this outcome of furthering comprehension and exploration has to be the Dialogist's intention, by which this Species is distinguished.

It now becomes possible to define *Nurture*, by contrast with *Evangelism*, making use of our definition of a committed Christian. *Nurture* is thus defined in terms of activities of communication which are intended to increase the depth and extent of a committed Christian's knowledge, faith, experience and practice: for the purposes of Nurturers and their intentions, the Communicatee's commitment is *now* presupposed. Thus it is clearly implied that, by requiring nurture to presuppose the subject of it is a committed Christian, it is not logically possible to nurture young children. Thus the enterprise of teaching the faith to the children of Christian parents or to other children in the milieu of the church is another distinct endeavour, for which we introduce the term '*Child Nurture*'.

Child Nurture can thus be specified as another species of Communication. This species may be defined as the evangelism of children, conducted over the years of childhood, with the likely result that when they are mature enough, the young people those children grow up into, become committed Christians. In terms of our earlier definitions most such children will already be Christians through Infant Baptism, Dedication or whatever; and they may well be practising Christians because they worship. *Child Nurture* is evangelistic in that it may result in autonomous commitment at the appropriate age of maturity. Clearly such *Child Nurture* will have to comprise different sub-activities at the different ages and stages of childhood,[6] taking account of what is known of child-development and of the overriding procedural moral value of respect for persons.[7] The *Child Nurturer's* intention will be so to communicate the faith in childhood that a free and responsible commitment will be reached one day but not before adulthood is attained.

The Species of Communication which is Religious Education may be defined as it is in the Schools Curriculum and Assessment Authority's Model Syllabuses (the product of a semi-official government agency). The crucial section of its statement of the aims of Religious Education says: 'Religious Education should help pupils to: .. acquire and develop the ability to make reasoned and informed judgements about religious and moral issues with reference to the teachings of the principal religions represented in Great Britain'.[8]

Such an enterprise will be governed by the values and conceptual requirements of education: for education by its very nature is the initiation of students into worthwhile knowledge in a worthwhile way, respecting the reason and integrity of the pupils.[9] Respect will have to be shown to children as moral agents free to explore all the major faiths of the world (which happily coincide with those represented in Great Britain). Religious Education will try to cover the beliefs, myths, symbols, practices and values of those religions. Its effect will be to open up the religious dimension for the pupil and to generate in him or her sufficient interest and empathy for a personal voyage of discovery across the sea of faith. The end result intended, unlike *Evangelism* and *Nurture*, is open-ended, not predetermined, because Religious Education belongs to education in a controversial area. Religious Education will be successful when the student reaches an informed and reasonable position, positive or negative, with or without commitment, towards the major religions which constitute the subject-matter of this part of the curriculum. And such a position is the end state the educator intends to produce.

Our Theory will also apply to the *Academic Study of Religion*. This can be defined as that communicative discipline in Higher Education (or schools) which has the religions of the world as its subject-matter approached in a scholarly way. Unlike Religious Education, which seeks to promote broad understanding and exploration as part of a liberal or general education, academic study of anything is training in scholarship, which may lead at the postgraduate level to the student being able to become a scholar in the appropriate discipline. It is presupposed that the student has made a voluntary choice of his or her subject of study and has the motivation to study successfully. It does indeed intend, like Religious Education, to inform, to encourage exploration and perhaps to reach a reasonable assessment of the faith(s) studied. But the objective is not commitment to a faith, nor is this presupposed. One mark of successful teaching of religion as an academic discipline is that it is fertilised by research and scholarship, that students are motivated to continue to be aware of research and scholarship, and even to pursue these for their own sake.

Finally we can see *Ministerial Formation* as yet another application of our Theory and definable in terms of it. This process is the training required to be a religious professional, a priest, clergy-person, minister, pastor, a full- or part-time worker in a religious community, who evangelise or nurture others in the community's faith. (By Minister, clearly we do *not* mean a *Religious Education* teacher or an academic working in the *Academic Study of Religion*.) *Ministerial Formation* can be regarded as a combination of *Nurture* and the *Academic Study of Religion*.

Clearly *Nurture* is involved for it builds on being a committed Christian (or other faith follower). Only such a person can with integrity teach a particular faith as true and work effectively for the faith-community over a life time, as a career or at least for a substantial period. Lacking such commitment, a minister is either an hypocrite, or has such a fluctuating and variable belief, that they will be unable to sustain their occupation over time. The Communicator's intention is to produce in the Minister a commitment to explore and to go on exploring his or her existing faith and thereby to deepen it.

Yet such a person's commitment needs to be founded upon and nourished by an extensive and profound academic study of his or her own faith (and nowadays the faith of others). Therefore this *Nurture* must take place within Higher Education and also has to belong to the *Academic Study of Religion*. Such a programme of study will necessarily involve critical scrutiny of the potential minister's deepest beliefs and the temporary suspension or bracketing of commitment, while in the classroom and when in debate. It is desirable, if not essential, as we shall see later,[10] that this exploration occurs in the 'open' context of Higher Education, at times in discussion with other students and teachers of any or no personal commitment, as well at other times with the support of his or her co-religionists. Thus *Ministerial Formation* belongs to Higher Education but differs from the *Academic Study of Religion* in intending Commitment; and the kind of Commitment intended is distinct from the initial commitment to a particular faith which is the end-state the *Evangelist* aims at and is more specialised than that which *Nurture* has as its objective.

In these ways our seven Species of Communication have been distinguished from one another by the Communicator's intention. Now these intentions have been specified by their content. It has to be noted that these end-states aimed at are not mutually exclusive: a Communicatee may come to understand and to explore religion and also may reach or retain positive faith commitment. Despite the teacher's or professor's intention a student in school *Religious Education* or in Higher Education's *Academic Study of Religion* may incidentally come to commitment. Does this raise a problem for our account? If we had distinguished our Species purely by the outcome, and not by the intention, then could not *Religious Education* and *the Academic Study of Religion* be regarded as *Evangelism*?

When such an unforeseen outcome is occasionally produced, this result is quite consistent with an intentional account. For agents do not always realise their intentions or may achieve further end-states beyond their original aim. Such incidental results are no great problem. But suppose a *Religious Education* teacher or a Religious Studies or Theology professor regularly brought about positive faith commitment in his or her students? In human activity, one presumes agents frequently or usually achieve certainly their professed aims, by which their actions are individuated. But a widespread divergence of the outcome from the Communicator's avowed and professed intention conflicts with the commonsense and legal principle that agents intend the reasonable and natural consequences of their actions. In the cases supposed we might think the teacher or professor really had an unavowed, implicit or unconscious intention to evangelise. They could be asked to review their approach and either to change it or to admit their enterprise should be reclassified as another Species in our list. In such ways what we actually find to be the outcomes reached can be made consistent with our differentiation of the Species of Religious Communication by the Communicator's intention.

(iv) Assumptions of the Theory

We have described how our Theory came about and we have defined and clarified some of the key concepts we are concerned with. Now, finally, in this Introduction we set out the basic assumptions we make about our society in the UK and in much of the West generally in a secular age and our postulates about the nature of religion, in particular Christianity.

Christianity, first, has to be communicated in a social context. And the social context the Theory is designed to fit is that of a Secular Age, not of Christendom. We have to communicate to people not normally socialised into Christianity or into any other faith by their upbringing, nor pressurised into religious conformity by the teachers, authorities, media, opinion-formers and the social climate of our world. There is no general societal 'plausibility structure' to maintain faith today.[11] Practising Christians are a minority in England,[12] even more so adherents of other religions.[13]

The British nation has a Christian past but this is fast fading.[14] Education cannot take for granted a national Christian heritage, despite the 1988 Education Reform Act and Circular1/94,[15] which enacted Religious Education as part of the basic curriculum of English schools and which prescribed religious worship for the pupils. Apart from a few children from Christian homes or who have lived in a church milieu, or who belong to ethnic minority groups, adults grow up with little religious background the Communicator can work upon. Today, whatever may have been the case in the early years of the twentieth century, a religious outlook or church allegiance is not taken in and absorbed with one's mother's milk. Moreover, it is not at all easy to generate an interest in a dimension simply missing from most people's everyday lives.[16] It is in this society that our Theory applies: in other circumstances it would be inapplicable or otiose.

Second we assume British society (or any other to which our Theory will apply) is pluralistic, in that other world faiths are represented here and the choice between religion for adults is a real one. Citizens can choose a faith, convert freely from one religion to another, and can expect pastoral support in hospital or prison, without running into persecution, opposition or social pressure against apostatising, as in many other places. Indeed most people in our society, whom we call non-practising, or even aborted Christians, have no real spiritual position to apostatise from. Religious communication today cannot be of one faith presented in isolation from all others, certainly if truth and the person of the Communicatee is to be respected and information given which fairly reflects the nature of religion. In Religious Education, the S.C.A.A. documents of an official British governmental agency and the 1988 Act[17] of the English Parliament make requirements and imply values, which the other Species of Religious Communication also can hardly fail to embody – if these values are also implicit in the Christian religion[18] and in other faiths.

The third assumption we make, in addition to secularity and pluralism, is that coming to an adult faith in our society must be a matter of personal choice. Communication needs motivation, a chance to become informed, an opportunity for exploration and a free coming, if at all, to a rational commitment. Indoctrination of any type is excluded: and we understand by this vexed and contested concept forms of teaching that bring about in a person a state of belief and commitment beyond the reach of criticism and revision.[19] Not only do educational premisses forbid indoctrination, but the Christian Gospel, by its respect for truth, integrity and the conscience of the individual, also prohibits the *Evangelist* and *Nurturer* from this propagandist practice.[20] (Our Theory assumes other faiths also have this concern about the manner of their propagation.)

Our Theory is designed to help people to think for themselves, to encourage and to motivate young and old not to give undue weight to their tradition, peers, parents or to their own personal identity, as shaped prior to exposure to a religious message. Choice is not easy or natural in our society, even the choice to continue in the faith of one's fathers and mothers, and those who value autonomous choice must give support to individuals to resist the pressures to conform in the contemporary world.[21]

Fourthly and lastly one crucial assumption is made about Christianity and any other religion our Theory will apply to. This assumption concerns the 'what' of what is to be communicated. It is taken for granted that Christianity (or whatever) has at its heart a message, a content, a gospel, a proclamation or a theology that has to be put into words and statements, which in turn necessarily employ concepts. What is to be presented cannot be offered naked, without being clothed in some linguistic dress. We recognise that there are many different formulations of the Christian or other faith story: some offer it as objective and public truth about the universe;[22] some as a narrative that makes sense of our lives or as a perspective we may take up.[23]

The same goes for both realist and non-realist versions of religion,[24] although as we shall see, there is a crucial difference in how exploration proceeds in such cases. On non-realist accounts to explore is to consider subjectively whether a faith is personally attractive and illuminating. On a realist view exploration must include, as well as this subjective assessment, evaluation of the truth-claims a religion makes by some rationally defensible criteria that can apply to the various world-faiths.[25] Our Theory is neutral as between these possible interpretations and accounts of religion.

What this fourth assumption does exclude is that from the point of view of Communication and epistemology, Christianity is primarily a personal relationship with God or Christ.[26] Important as it is to receive God or Jesus as a person and to enter into a friendship with him, this is a development in faith, which presupposes a framework of belief expressed in language and responded to as true or as appropriate in some way. For the claim that one is in a personal relationship with a divine person is incoherent, without such a description as creed or doctrine gives of this phenomenon being true, and without a person's prior acceptance of the belief in its truth in the normal range of cases. The integrity of communication demands the respondent first assents to the propositional underpinning of the gospel to which he or she then reacts in this particular existential way.

Thus we complete the account of the assumptions of our Theory. When these are added to our earlier definitions and distinctions, the way is left clear to begin to construct our scheme.

Notes

[1] Within theology this work may be considered the *last* logical stage of Communications: v. Lonergan, B. (1972), *Method in Theology,* Darton, Longman and Todd, London, **14**.

[2] *Waiting on God* (1950), (E.T. Craufurd, E.), Collins Fontana, London, 13–25.

[3] *Stages of Faith* (1981), Harper Row, San Francisco.

[4] Abraham, W. J. (1989), *The Logic of Evangelism*, Hodder & Stoughton, London, 95–98.

[5] Ibid. 108–116.

[6] *All God's Children* (1992) (G.S. 988), National Society, London, 41, **5**.

[7] Peters, R. S. (1966), *Ethics and Education*, Allen and Unwin, 35–43, 208–215; Downie, R. S. and Telfer, E. (1969), Allen & Unwin, London, **1, 2, 5**.

[8] Schools Curriculum and Assessment Authority (1994), *Model Syllabuses for Religious Education Consultation Document, C.O.I.*, Introduction, **2.2,** 2.

[9] Peters op. cit. **!, 2**; *The Concept of Education* (1967), Routledge and Kegan Paul, **1**.

[10] v. **8** (iii).

[11] Berger, P. L. (1973), *The Social Reality of Religion*, Penguin Books, London, 54–60, 130–131, 138–139.

[12] In 1989 adult churchgoers were 9.5% of the adult population: Brierley, P. (1991), *Christian England*, London, 30; Gill, R. (1993), *The Myth of the Empty Church*, S.P.C.K., London, **10** Tables 272ff. The most recent statistics are that weekly attendance is now 7.5%, but perhaps 15% are in some degree of contact with the worshipping community: Brierley, P. (2000), *The Tide is Running Out,* Christian Research, London, 71–79.

[13] Badham, P. Ed. (1989), *Religion, State and Society in Modern Britain*, Edwin Mellen Press, Lampeter, **12–16**.

[14] Ibid., Smart, N., Church, Party and State, **20**; Berger op. cit. **5, 6**; Davie, G. (1994), *Religion in Britain since 1945*, Blackwell Oxford, **4, 5, 6**; Bruce, F. (1995), *Religion in Modern Britain*, O. U. P, Oxford, **2**.

[15] *The Educational Reform Act 1988*,ss 2(1), 8(3) and *Religious Education and Collective Worship*, Circular 1/94, Department for Education, London, §§ **7, 16**.

[16] v (11) and also the careful discussion of Mitchell, B. (1994), in *Faith and Criticism*, Clarendon Press, Oxford, **8**.

[17] s 8(3); S.C.A.A. op. cit.,1–3, §§ **1&2**

[18] Oman, J. (1925), *Grace and Personality*, C. U. P., 3rd Ed., 51–53, 61, 136–137, 140–143; also Abbott and Gallagher (1965), *The Documents of Vatican II*, G. Chapman, London, 689-690, **10**; Hodgson, L. (1968*), For Faith and Freedom*, S.C.M. Press, London, vol. I, 180–191, 203–207, 222, 224–228; vol. II 162–170, 178, 188–189, 221–223.

[19] White, J. (1967), Indoctrination, **11**, 177–191 in Peters op. cit.; Snook, I. A. (1972), *Indoctrination and Education*, and Ed. *Concepts of Indoctrination*, Routledge and Kegan Paul, London; Thiessen E. J., (1993), *Teaching for Commitment*, Gracewing, Leominster, 232–242.

[20] Thiessen op. cit., 136-140.

[21] Cf. Jonathan, R. (1995), Education and Moral Development: the role of reason and circumstance, in the *Journal of the Philosophy of Education*, **29. 3**, 1995, 333–354.

[22] Newbigin, L. (1983), *The Other Side of 84*, W.C.C. Geneva, 26–54, 60–62; (1986), *Foolishness to the* Greeks, S. P. C. K., **3**; (1989), *The Gospel in a Pluralist Society*, S. P. C. K. London, **1–5**; (1991)**,** *Truth to Tell***,** S. P. C. K.**,** London, **1**.

[23] Cupitt, D. (1989), *Radicals and the Future of the Church*, S.C.M. Press, London, **3, 4 & 6(e).**

[24] Runzo, J. Ed. (1993), *Is God Real?* Macmillan, London.

[25] v. **7** (iii).

[26] Astley, J. (2000), Aims and Approaches in Christian Education, in Astley, J. Ed., *Learning in the Way,* Gracewing, Leominister, 7–8, for a useful discussion of this difficult point.

Chapter 2

Current Forms of Religious Communication and Their Problems.

In this Chapter we consider attempts that have been made to communicate the Christian faith in the twentieth century in England as examples of contemporary religious communication and its problems. In this way it is hoped to cast light on religious communication in general by examining the attempts at communication by the Christian faith in a secular age.

We shall first outline the current decline in churchgoing and its causes and try to see this as a result of inability to communicate in the various forms distinguished in Chapter I. Then we shall examine how people do in fact normally come to faith and some of the factors involved in this process in the course of ordinary church life. Next we assess special efforts like crusade evangelism and focus on its differential success with various kinds of people.

This discussion leads on to one particular range of problems in communication, the relative lack of success with males as opposed to females, its causes and possible remedies. One new and interesting communicative enterprise is also explored and we analyse the conditions that make it effective. Finally the whole discussion is drawn together and we list what emerges from it as key considerations in religious communication today. Thus we lay the foundations for our general theory of religious communication that we hope will apply across all its particular Species, as already defined in Chapter I, and which will also apply across theistic faiths in secular societies in this new century.

(i) Church Decline and its Causes

We have already indicated the decline of Christianity in England over the past century.[1] There has been a steady, long-term decrease in regular churchgoing that we take as typical of religious life and as an index of how the churches have failed to nourish a common, popular and orthodox faith.[2]

Two principal explanations of this downward trend in worship and in faith have been offered by historians and sociologists. One account is the secularisation thesis. The churches have remained constant and presented a timeless message, but society has changed. The social climate is less religious, belief is harder, indifference has increased; and therefore people are less ready to respond to the communicative activities of the churches and so to attend regularly for worship, as indeed they gather together publicly less often today for any social purpose.

The other account is in terms of the churches over-expanding in the last half of the nineteenth century and throughout most of the twentieth. Over-expansion supposes that there exists a fixed quantity of potential churchgoers at any one time in the population; and this has been spread, by excessive church building, ever more thinly over multiplying places of worship, often even in the face of an absolute decrease in the populace in many areas. Hence congregations fall in numbers and then there are knock-on effects that ensure decline has continued for the next century (or in the case of the Roman Catholic church since the mid-twentieth century). Fewer worshippers than in the past in each place causes loss of morale and public confidence in the church; fewer ministers are appointed, whose work is more thinly stretched across congregations and thus less effective; inadequate giving makes institutional religion harder to sustain. The cumulative effect is long-term decline, whether in the rural setting of village depopulation or in large cities, where churches have spread to the suburbs and housing estates, without compensating closures of existing places of worship in inner and central districts.[3]

Which of these two major explanations of declining religious practice is the more plausible is not our concern. Both have obvious points in their favour and serious weaknesses. Our interest is in the claim that both explanations assume failure of the churches' communicative activities to maintain their strength. *Either* the Christian message has not been effectively presented to secularised people *or* the original and continuing churchgoing section of the population is not being maintained, still less enlarged, by successful evangelism or socialisation, whatever the changes in institutional structure on the ground.

This may be seen in terms of the seven Species of Religious Communication distinguished in Chapter I. Church decline reflects an obvious failure in *Evangelism* and in recruiting new committed believers and unsatisfactory *Child Nurture* of the children in touch with a congregation so that they are not held to faith or prepared for later adult receptivity to the preaching of the gospel. Again since much loss of numbers is due to worshippers lapsing, there has also been inadequate *Nurture* of adults, so that they resist the acids of apathy, ignorance and unbelief, when subjected to the depressing effects of immersion in dwindling congregations.

Clearly church decline may not be laid at the door of *Inter-Faith Dialogue,* since this has only been undertaken very recently in the last quarter of the twentieth century; has not been practised on a widespread scale in any area; and has not been pursued with an intention to convert, however crucial this form of communication may be to the future of faith in this twenty-first century, in the case of those coming from other religions.

Religious Education in schools used to aim at evangelism and nurture.[4] The evidence of the research of a generation ago found it had little success with these objectives.[5] But even when in the last forty years *Religious Education* has become open-ended and multi-faith, its general effect might have been expected to produce a population sympathetically disposed to the spiritual dimension, well-informed about religion and used to exploring faith. Such a crop of school leavers, so educated, should have formed favourable material for the church's message. Yet research suggests that even in its own terms contemporary *Religious Education* is far from receiving a favourable estimate from and being fruitful with many pupils[6] and will not thus in practice help indirectly with the church's communicative task.

Nor can the *Academic Study of Religion* nor *Ministerial Formation* totally escape some responsibility for the general decline of religion in England. Since many graduates of these species of communication have become church-workers or clergy (or rabbis and ministers of other faiths) their collective weaknesses in teaching successfully their congregations and the wider populace must be in part a product of their training.

Thus it seems that religious decline in twentieth century England may be attributed partly to failure across almost all the Species of our genus of Religious Communication.

(ii) The Normal Process of Communication

Most normal processes of religious communication have been the object of the research of Churches Together in England published in the book *Finding Faith Today.*[7] This project analysed the factors that brought all the new recruits into the mainstream English churches in 1991. So here we may see the positive effects of the several Denominations' routine attempts to pass on their message in their ordinary day to day activities up and down the country. Some of the findings of this enquiry are important in discovering what makes for success in *Evangelism* and *Nurture.*

The most outstanding discovery is that two thirds of the sample came to faith gradually, the average time taken being about 4 years.[8] While there was a minority of sudden conversions, becoming a worshipper, it seems, for most people is a long drawn-out process and therefore it may be concluded that communication cannot be done all at once. It further appears the new converts had first got to know church people, then began to worship and be familiar with church life, until eventually faith and commitment seemed to crystallise. Hence it should be possible to map out the stages in the communicative process: motivation by contact with existing Christian people; worship; exploration; and some sort of coming to commitment.

New recruits always begin with informal acquaintance and friendship with people in congregations, whose warmth and witness were crucial. Which people the first contacts were with varied by Denomination.[9] With the Free Churches initial encounter was with personal friends in the local church, often with those running organisations. With the Church of England it was often the Vicar people met in connection with the Occasional Offices. At times of sadness and joy, over funerals, baptisms and weddings, the clergy of the established church have unique opportunities to make contact in depth with non-churchgoers and to set up trusting relations with them. Roman Catholic first encounters were through marriage to non-Catholics. Over years of happy marriage and family life, the non-practising or nominal partner of another Denomination was inspired to learn, explore and eventually to reach faith.

Again the emphasis is on a process of time, in each of these forms of making and building contact. The warmth and witness of existing church people were central to motivating the secularised person to begin to be interested and to want to go further. It is obvious that a variety of Christians can be identified as crucial to these encounters and should be trained in the making of contact, while they go about their ordinary daily business. This appears to be a critical dimension of *Evangelism* and *Nurture*.

The importance of *Child Nurture* also emerges in *Finding Faith Today*.[10] Few people came to faith as adults who had not had significant contact with the church as children.[11] That childhood encounter was necessary but not sufficient for adult conversion. Good children's work seems to have to proceed on the assumption that when young people grow up, they will not stay in the faith community but that some of them can later be won back.

More may be learnt from this research finding. It points to the importance of Christian background for the new convert. He or she needs some foundation of knowledge – more than that, a positive attitude – to make them receptive to the gospel message, even simply in order to understand it. Should this youthful contact have been in church schools (or even in state schools?), perhaps it may be deduced that some level of general education, associated with religious learning, may be critical. Also it is worthy of note that attending schools – compulsory with ordinary day school or under parental pressure in times gone by for Sunday School – may have given the necessary opportunity to learn and explore, the time needed if communication is to be effective, a chance that is difficult for adults to have today amid all the pressures of modern life.

Thus ordinary church life indicates some of the ingredients of religious communication: learning and a chance to learn in childhood, motivation through human contact in later years; and time and leisure to find real faith, after traversing many steps on a long road.

(iii) A Special Process of Communication

On some occasions individual Christians or churches or voluntary Christian organisations have attempted to broadcast their message to whole populations in special campaigns. One variety of campaign is 'crusade evangelism'. Backed by mass publicity and local church support, a gifted preacher proclaims the gospel in a large stadium to a huge audience nightly for weeks and months, thus touching a significant fraction of the population. Such were the Billy Graham crusades of Mission England in the early 1980s, in major provincial cities, though not in London.[12] The results have been carefully recorded, published and analysed; they seem highly relevant to our discussion.

The numbers who came forward at these great rallies to profess or re-affirm faith were impressive.[13] More remarkable still is the fact that 80% of these persons already had a church connection.[14] This powerfully suggests that the address in the stadium at the meeting, however inspired, is only the last step in coming to faith. Reaching commitment is indeed important: however, earlier church-going, socialisation into a faith-community, learning, worship and exploration are also crucial in the total sequence that constitutes *Evangelism*. The support of a large crowd at the rally, being with friends on the coach on the way, even communal hymn- and chorus-singing, were also found to help maintain and increase motivation.[15]

Obviously there was a risk of emotional, immature and suggestible people deciding to go forward on impulse, without real thought, not understanding what they were doing. This great danger, which exists despite the need of enthusiasm to make persons move out of their inertia and complacency, points nonetheless to a need for the Communicatee to be able and disposed to decide for Christ *autonomously*. Now if a normal upbringing and schooling do not develop rational autonomy, perhaps the Communicator should regard it as part of his or her business to teach thinking for oneself and not being dominated by social, family or ethnic tradition, prejudice or peer pressure. A liberal education should foster rational autonomy, but it does no harm and much good to include it in the process of religious communication as a preparation for learning and exploration.

Another striking research finding from the Graham crusade was its differential record of success with some social groups rather than others.[16] Those responding were heavily weighted towards females, the young and middle class, as opposed to males, older folk, the unemployed or unskilled.[17] Any rational theory of communication must pay attention to such factors if it is to be of guidance in approaching everyone in a secular age.

The age of response might be influenced by opportunity to attend. This could be easier for younger than for older people with family and work commitments. Many factors may be relevant here, and there is a need for opportunity to be offered in many different ways and forms to Communicatees in widely divergent situations. Does communication require travel, attendance at large evening rendezvous? Why not at home, via electronic media, on the Internet etc.?

As for sex and class, wide differences in response to religion and its communication, not only in the case of Mission England but much more generally, are well-known.[18] The causes are much less clear. We do not discuss here the explanation of social class differences in religious behaviour and their relevance to the Theory we hope to build, because there is no general agreement on why class divergences in religious behaviour are so marked. There has been much discussion of the alienation of the working-class from the churches at the Industrial Revolution, yet this alienation was two centuries ago! We may speculate on a range of factors operating today in maintaining this effect, like continuing social tradition, poverty, low educational attainment, lack of propensity to be 'joiners', absence of autonomy, want of opportunity through scanty leisure, even in the present age. Any or all of these considerations may impede the effectiveness of communication. In constructing our Theory we shall try to take account of this problem by putting forward what we shall call Background Conditions of Religious Communication, which comprehensively cover what, in the writer's experience and thinking, are at any rate of some importance in this area.[19]

In the case of gender, however, enough is known of the causes of differential response to religion to merit the separate discussion below.

(iv) Gender and Communication

There is a major difference between the sexes in religious behaviour.[20] Women responded in much greater numbers to Billy Graham and are found in much greater numbers in churches.[21] From this fact we may presume in some way they are more receptive to religious communication. Why such differences occur and what should be done to communicate more effectively with men and boys is the topic of this section of our discussion.

An important piece of research recently conducted by Leslie Francis and Carolyn Wilcox finds the explanation to lie mainly in divergent personality structure, in the distinction between characteristic masculine and feminine qualities.[22] Femininity consists, in the operational definition used, of being yielding, shy, affectionate, loyal, sympathetic and understanding. Masculinity similarly comprises being self-reliant, independent, assertive, forceful and analytical.[23] It appears that being feminine makes it easier to respond to and receive the Christian message, whereas the faith seems less congruous with the masculine qualities just mentioned. Granted on the whole males are masculine and females feminine, the gender difference in religious response is explained. An interesting exception is the feminine personality found in clergy who are mainly male - the exception that proves the rule![24] Other factors like sex role expectancy played no significant part in predicting the variance among the sixth form and student populations studied (16-20's) but retained some weight with younger secondary pupils (13-15).[25]

There is no certainty that this explanation covers the data found in other studies of other groups. The samples studied by Francis and Wilcox are not representative of the whole population: older and younger ages are not covered; those outside the limits of higher education and sixth form could respond religiously by gender for other reasons. In the absence of wider research samples, it is reasonable to take account of parish experience that points to lower levels of literacy and ability to handle words as playing a part with males in the lower socio-economic groups. OFSTED data from schools, admittedly at the Primary stage, finds boys to be less literate than girls in Key Stage 2 SATS[26] and so to find it harder to accept the verbal aspect of a faith largely and necessarily expressed in books and writing.

What should be done to overcome such problems in religious communication? Obviously further research is needed to test the personality or gender orientation theory on samples representative of the entire population of modern secular societies. In the meantime, given the plausibility of Francis and Wilcox's research for a large and significant section of Communicatees, two alternative approaches are suggested to tackle the problem.

Either motivation to respond positively to religion and to its communication can be improved by stressing to men and boys the masculine aspect of faith e.g. the heroic qualities of Jesus and the saints or by emphasising rational apologetics which appeal to the more analytic element in the masculine personality orientation. It is interesting to note how Industrial Chaplains used to say that, once the ice is broken with working-men, vigorous argument about all manner of questions, including religious ones, is the order of the day.

Or the alternative strategy is to change the Communicatee, to bring up boys to be more feminine, as the clergy already are. It is important to note that masculinity and femininity are not mutually exclusive and indeed that both can be present to a high degree in a balanced personality.[27] Changing patterns of socialisation will make boys become more truly autonomous when they grow into men, not being so prejudiced from infancy against religion as soft and sissy.

Finally, should there be anything in explaining male lack of religiosity by want of verbal ability, then this element needs attention in any theory of religious communication; and the same goes for any other differential factors in sex or class responsiveness to religion. Compensatory treatment is required as part of adequate presentation of the gospel to such a group or groups in the population.

(v) A New Positive Approach

So far our discussion has been largely negative, stressing the problems and difficulties of religious communication. Now we examine the relevance to the Theory we are trying to build of 'Natural Church Development',[28] a new strategy that has recently emerged to promote church growth. After extensive research across the world and across all major Christian traditions, C. Schwarz has found that the numerical growth of a congregation correlates significantly to the quality of its community life.[29] On the assumption that expansion of the worshipping community, if only to counter natural losses due to ageing, death and moving away, requires *Evangelism, Nurture* and *Child Nurture,* it follows that the qualitative dimensions of church activity and experience must assist religious communication.

Schwarz has constructed an instrument to measure the quality of a congregation's life and worship, a questionnaire which has to be completed by the minister and thirty of the congregation. When processed the data yield scores in eight dimensions of quality.[30] These are: *empowering leadership,* to identify the gifts of members of the congregation and to encourage them to develop these talents; *gift-orientated lay ministry,* on the part of the congregation willing to be trained in using its gifts on behalf of the church; *passionate spirituality,* where people pray with enthusiasm; *functional structures,* these being an organisational structure in a community that does not rely on purely spiritual factors, a structure that is not antiquated and serves effectively present day needs; *inspiring worship service,* where everyone enjoys services and does not attend out of a sense of duty alone, despite boredom; *holistic small groups,* which embrace a significant fraction of the congregation, making regularly for friendship, mutual support, sharing troubles, as well as for prayer and study; *need-orientated evangelism,* everyone witnessing, but those gifted for evangelism giving a lead in approaching non-Christians' individual needs; and *loving relationships,* in a congregation, where there is laughter and mutual socialising, not just while in church. When a local church is assessed on these eight dimensions and scores an average quality index of 65 (above a median 50 mark) across the dimensions, there is a strong empirical probability of growth;[31] and therefore, in our terms of being able to communicate effectively, assuming that this leads people to attend church.

Next we must see what are the key factors in these dimensions of congregational quality that make for effective communication and which need addressing in our Theory. The dimensions of *empowering leadership, gift-orientated lay ministry* and *functional structures* seem to lack an obvious direct relevance to communication but perhaps they bring about a general effectiveness in a local church in any tasks it undertakes; also these dimensions indicate that minister and people, or some of them, are equipped and trained for religious communication in particular.

Inspiring worship service and *passionate spirituality* are important in a secular age for making God real for people, first for the Communicators and then through them and their influence to the Communicatees, giving these latter the ability to respond to the message and to take it seriously. *Need-orientated evangelism* and *loving relationships* help generate interest and motivation in the secular community, when it sees evident non-religious needs being addressed and local people in the community feeling welcome and cared for. If the biggest hurdle to get over is motivation to be open to religion in a social climate of apathy, then these dimensions are critical.

Holistic small groups may be the most important factor of all. Not only do such groups assist in producing a generally positive attitude to faith, but they enable the Communicatees to appreciate that, while they share so much with the rest of the group, they lack its religious awareness. Consequently the Communicatees feel the need to overcome this gap between themselves and the rest and to remove any discrepancy between their own belief-system and that of the Communicators. Thus the Communicatees may come to desire to bring their own creed, attitude and values into line with the others in the holistic group. This may turn out to be the absolutely crucial factor which makes a person want to learn about and explore a faith.

(vi) The Requirements of Communication

The time has come at last to draw together the threads of this extensive discussion of various contemporary approaches to religious communication and to see which factors are important and need to be built in to a comprehensive account of the Communicator's task. To realise just what steps are required and to order them in logical sequence will then, when this section is complete, be the work of the next Chapter in constructing our Core Theory.

It has emerged from the preceding sections that certain conditions in the Communicatee need to be established, possibly by the Communicator, before communication can begin. These requirements should receive attention in their own right and before presenting the message commences. The Communicatee must be made ready to receive the message. For this three 'background' conditions appear to be necessary.

First to the extent a religion has an inescapably verbal message to pass, and which cannot be simplified beyond a certain point without critical loss, the Communicatee needs to be educated and to develop a certain ability with words in childhood or subsequently. Second in childhood (if not later) the person, who it is hoped will one day to be able to respond to the gospel, must be equipped with autonomy, so as, on the one hand not to take claims too readily for granted and on the other, not to close their mind to what their home and culture may reject. Various prejudices want anticipating and removing in advance, so that these do not constitute fatal obstacles later in the communication process. Thus this enterprise of fostering autonomy is also within the Communicator's remit.

The third responsibility of the Communicator is to organise occasions when a person has opportunity to hear the message (or read or watch a film or TV). This organisation has to take account of the exigencies of much adult life and its pressures and also the chances of communication in childhood, schooling, youth and the student phase of growing up. Perhaps because these youthful opportunities are so rich, we may assume that comparable ones are much harder to find in later life. Yet the special chances that arise of hearing the message in age, leisure or in the forced leisure of unemployment must not be neglected.

The direct process of communication itself clearly involves learning and exploration. These take time and however much is done in childhood, the whole enterprise needs to provide for the processes also to occur in maturity, as a preface to urging properly adult commitment. It is important to identify what has to be learned as a minimum that is practicable for everyone. Also the subjective and objective aspects of exploration, the appeal to the various aspects of people's needs and aspirations, and also evaluation of the truth-claims of faith, need providing for and setting out.

Above all, motivation is central to the direct process of communication, when opportunity for it to happen has been made available. Otherwise the chance will not be taken, attention and participation will not be sustained. We have seen how a sympathetic, caring approach by the Communicator is the first step, which needs to be maintained over the whole time this complex enterprise takes. Yet something more is needed. In a secular age motivation will not be sufficient unless the whole religious or godward dimension is taken seriously, and something has to be done to counter indifference and the notion people hold of a god who is neither real nor important. Once again prior changes are required in the outlook of the Communicatee before he or she will seriously listen and be moved to respond, and these are the duty of the Communicator to promote.

Hence when we construct our Core Theory in the next Chapter, we shall have to fit together in a logical order background factors; programmes of learning and exploration and the chance to become committed; and preceding this direct phase of the whole procedure, a time to invoke social forces that stimulate motivation and generate a sense of God's reality.

Notes

[1] v. **1** (iv).
[2] v. **1** (10).
[3] Gill, op. cit., Introduction, 272–275.
[4] Compare "The first principle then, underlying the following syllabus, is that the primary function of religious teaching is to show the way in which Christianity offers the right relationship between God and man ... the chief task of the school is to train for Christian citizenship" ((1957), *The Middlesex County Agreed Syllabus of Religious Instruction,* Middlesex County Council, London, 12) *with* "Religious Education should help pupils to acquire and develop knowledge and understanding of Christianity and the other principle religions represented in Great Britain ... develop reasoned and informed

judgements about religious and moral issues" ((1995), *Durham County Council Agreed Syllabus for Religious Education,* Durham, 2).

[5] Loukes, H. (1965), *New Ground in Christian Education*, S.C.M. Press, London, **5, 6, Appendixes A, B, C.**

[6] Francis, L. J. (1996), Who wants RE? a Sociopsychological profile of adolescent support for Religious *Education,* in Astley, J. and Francis, L. J. Eds., *Christian Theology and Religious Education,* S. P. C. K., London, **14**.

[7] Finney, J. (1992),British and Foreign Bible Society, Swindon.

[8] Op. cit., **3**.

[9] Ibid. **4, 5.**

[10] Ibid. **2**.

[11] Ibid. 12.

[12] Black, P. (1985), *mission: england*, Marc Europe, London.

[13] Ibid., 4.

[14] Ibid., 30–32, 42–45.

[15] Ibid., 17, 63.

[16] Ibid., 22–42

[17] Ibid., 36–42.

[18] Argyle, M. and Beit-Hallahmi, B. (1975), *The Social Psychology of Religion,* Routledge and Kegan Paul, London, **5, 10**; Bruce, op. cit., 42–44.

[19] v. 3 (iii), **4**.

[20] Argyle and Beit-Hallahmi, op. cit., **5.**

[21] Brierley, op. cit., 79–92.

[22] Francis, L. J. and Wilcox, C. (1996), Religion and Gender Orientation, *Personality and Individual Differences,* **20**,119–121, [a]; (1998), Religiosity and Femininity: Do Women really hold a more positive attitude to Christianity, *Journal for the Scientific Study of Religion,* **37**(3): 462–469, [b].

[23] [b] 464.

[24] [a] 120.

[25] [b] 464–467.

[26] OFSTED, *Primary Education: Review of Primary Schools in England 1994–98,* **3.1**, Chart 12, 13.

[27] [a] 119; [b] 463, 466.

[28] Schwarz, C. (1996), *Natural Church Development,* (UK Ed.), British Church Growth Association, Moggerhanger.

[29] Ibid., 20–21, 38–48.

[30] Ibid., 22–37.

[31] Ibid., 40–41.

Chapter 3

The Core Theory

In this Chapter we shall derive a four-stage Model conceived to help conceptualise Religious Education and claim for this Model a wider usefulness within our General Theory of Religious Communication. Then we shall add a further stage to make a five-stage Model and clarify what is meant by a stage-model. Finally we shall revise the Theory, re-presenting it from the Communicator's standpoint and thus come up with our definitive eight-stage Model.

(i) The Four-Stage Model

Religious communication in its various forms aims for or allows the possibility of Commitment as its final result. But before a person can be properly committed, are there any preconditions to be satisfied? Since religion is controversial, and if the whole process of communication has to be governed by the moral value of respect for persons, as we have seen,[1] Commitment has to be preceded by Exploration. The Communicatees need to investigate religious questions for themselves and reach their own conclusions. Only then is it proper for them to commit themselves to what they now think is true. Thus a moral argument requires the final stage of Commitment to be preceded by a stage of Exploration.

It is a logical point that you cannot rationally and effectively explore if you are ignorant of the main facts, including the principal points in controversy and the arguments usually advanced. Since in contemporary society the majority of people have no religious background and are therefore ignorant of these facts, points and arguments (or are certainly uninformed about any faiths other than their own family's), a stage of Learning before Exploration is required.

Now Learning needs activity or work on the part of the learner. Whether it be listening attentively to a lecture, talk or sermon or reading a book or watching a film, heed must be given and attention shown. Students or pupils will not participate in discussion unless they want to and are prepared to try to understand and grasp the issues. Hence the need for interest to be generated and motivation to be supplied. To create motivation we postulate a stage of Motivation to be undertaken as a distinct and conscious enterprise. Thus we reach our Four-Stage Model of Motivation, Learning, Exploration and Commitment.

The type of argument used to justify Exploration before Commitment is moral, as we have seen above. Conceptual or logical arguments however are needed to derive the second stage from the third and the first from the second. Exploration, in a literal sense, of virgin territory is finding out the lie of the land, so as to replace ignorance by knowledge. But, in education and communication, exploration is a metaphor for investigation in a controversial area and consists in discussing, debating, testing and weighing arguments, exercising judgement and combining considerations.[2] This task cannot be effectively accomplished in ignorance of what in a controversy is held to be established.

Again in the argument that Learning needs Motivation, there is a conceptual link between the achievement of the knowledge or belief to be learnt and the task of doing whatever effects learning, and a further link connects this doing with motivation for doing it. Apart from curiosity as a motivation for working – when this natural trait exists – people do not do anything except for a reason, so sustained work needs motivation to be provided for the Communicatee.

(ii) Adding the Fifth Stage

It is a truism that motivation is to give someone a reason to act. In religion we commonly exclude the motivation of self-interest, as not often being present and also as morally doubtful. Learning religious facts to avoid hell and to gain heaven does not appeal to the contemporary Communicator as a form of motivation for him or her to appeal to: and such 'prudential' considerations would be ineffective ex hypothesi with those not religious. Clearly they will feel no duty of any sort to study a faith. What remains for communication is to find some way of interesting the Communicatee in religion.

Now a major way to interest anyone in any topic is to find an approach beginning in a familiar field or area, where the person to be interested feels personally involved; and in that field or area, that the learner thinks is important, to introduce puzzles, questions, paradoxes and contradictions challenging the learner's preconceptions. For 'cognitive dissonance', as this conflict of cognitions is termed, arises when a new thought clashes with existing beliefs, weighted by their importance to the believer.[3] The problem with motivating secular people for religious learning is that they have no prior awareness of the importance of religious faith. For to become interested in religious matters a person must already be involved in the Godward dimension as something weighty and significant to them and that means already to be religious. This is why so much religious communication fails, when this dimension is absent from someone's consciousness.

For example, young people may be interested in sport and a Christian sportsman or woman is brought in to testify to the gospel. So long as he or she keeps to the language of sport, progress is made, but when God is spoken of, a new sphere is entered and interest fades. Or a Christian works alongside non-committed people to tackle some common social or world problem. Provided the topic is approached on secular lines and the language of pragmatics or of humanist rational ethics is used – say employing utilitarian arguments – both sides keep their enthusiasm, find a common goal and are moved to joint action. But the Christian may be disappointed that the non-Christian is rarely led by his or her Christian witness during their joint endeavours, in such a way as to become interested in the Christian faith.

In our culture religion is a private affair and, in the world's eye, has only an optional connection to action in the public sphere.[4] You can find a good reason for working towards peace, social justice or greening the environment, which appeals to believer and unbeliever alike, without dragging God in, if God is not there already and does not feature in people's grounds for concern. The public debate on what to do in politics, culture and public affairs can proceed for ever without drawing in religious considerations. The good pagan and the Christian have reasons enough in common to co-operate. What privately means so much to the man or woman of faith is their own affair and arouses no interest in the secular person.

Nor is interest necessarily aroused in the beneficiaries of religious social action. Christians may strive for social righteousness and the realisation of the kingdom in contemporary society, by voluntary work or by political activity. The hungry are fed, the homeless housed, refugees receive a welcome, the unemployed are given employment, and worthwhile leisure is organised by Christian bodies for bored and alienated youth. But experience shows that the gratitude, which may be genuinely felt by the recipients of charity or social welfare work, does not automatically change into interest in the faith of the religious enthusiasts who give a lead or support such Christian action.

Perhaps people in a society with a Christian tradition expect the church to be concerned with social problems and to be compassionate. Religious people are indeed criticised for hypocrisy if they are indifferent to poverty and injustice. There may also sometimes be curiosity into what motivates the saints who sacrifice money and leisure to help their neighbours. But in a secular age, where the godward dimension is foreign to a normal outlook, this expectation of help and curiosity about what moves those who do give aid of any kind, does not normally or naturally or easily lead to wanting to learn about the faith of those who work for the good of their fellows from more than human sympathy and kindness.

It follows then that a distinctive religious motivation is needed in those who are non-religious. How then can the Communicatee be led into a charmed circle of faith? It is, of course, true that for children and some adults non-religious motivations to study faith can sometimes occur. Natural curiosity, in the young and occasionally in the old, is sometimes excited by the more colourful phenomena of a religion, especially when it is not one's own. But the scope for this is limited as adolescents grow up in a secular culture.[5] In education and higher education students may be motivated to study religion to pass exams for the sake of their careers. However, neither curiosity nor self-interest are likely to generate the high and sustained level of real interest that religious communication demands.

What we have to do is to divide the motivation of people into two phases. Before trying any of the myriad recipes for interesting Communicatees that ingenuity can devise, we need to prepare the ground by generating awareness of God. People today may claim to be theists, though beneath the surface of their avowals, there may be more unbelievers in God than one would at first suspect.[6] But the theism of the majority is too thin and vague, and their conception of the divine will not carry enough weight for religious issues to be psychologically real and meaningful to them. Hence the Stage of Motivation needs to be prepared for by a further preliminary stage in our Theory, a Stage of Nourishing the Sense of God.[7]

So we complete our First Model of Religious Communication for theistic faith in a secular age. The first model of our final theory has five stages: Nourishing the Sense of God, Motivation, Learning, Exploring and Commitment. It is, however, important, before proceeding any further, to be clear about the nature of our Theory. It is not an explanatory theory in psychology, like Fowler or Kohlberg,[8] showing how an end-stage is attained by a fixed, universal and progressive sequence of earlier logical or temporal stages, empirically discriminated. Our Theory is rather a practical theory of the order of steps to be taken to achieve a given result by an agent. Such steps are not established by psychological research as in stage-cognitive theories but by moral, logical or conceptual arguments and the commonsense of practical reason.

Our steps are not necessarily temporally discrete, nor of significant temporal duration. What *is* claimed is that the task represented by a prior stage must be carried out to a certain degree before the next can usefully get under way. Beware of the fallacy of the so-called 'perfected steps',[9] which requires that a step or stage in a learning or cognitive sequence needs completing or perfecting before the learner can begin to enter the next. And indeed no independent criterion can be given for the satisfaction of the prior need, apart from the readiness to begin the next step, so the prior stage cannot in any case be known to be perfected in itself. Rather we claim that the earlier step cannot begin after the latter has started. In fact our stages overlap and can be largely contemporaneous. In principle reading a book could cover the whole process of communication as it has been set out up to now.

Indeed our stages are largely cumulative and the enterprise each represents contributes to progress through all the successive stages. So throughout Religious Communication, motivation must continue to be provided; learning and motivation reinforce each other; new data energise fresh investigation; and new questions demand more facts. Theological exploration can go on indefinitely and Communicatees may never proceed to commit themselves; further distinct encouragement is then needed for them to transform tentative conclusions into the commitment of faith. There may also be temporal gaps between stages, especially with children, where further advances may wait on attaining maturity. An adult may go so far in the Learning or Exploring stages and then stop, resume and only after an interval begin seriously to consider Commitment.

(iii) The Background Conditions

Experience in urban parishes also suggests that further factors may govern the success of religious communication. There are psychological and social preconditions for the communicative process to flourish. So from these considerations we derive what we shall term *Background Conditions,* which are required if our first Five-Stage Model is to be successful.

The first Background Condition is *Verbal Ability.* Because a religion has a message formulated in propositions, it has a verbal content involving ideas and concepts. Hence a certain facility with words and ideas is needed in the Communicatees before they are able to receive profitably what is on offer.[10] Learning cannot come about except in terms of some formulation in words of what has to be grasped. Exploration clearly takes place in language and Commitment has to be made precise in forms like the vows in marriage, baptism or confirmation.

In practice it is hard to proceed far in religious communication without literacy. The whole enterprise will be vastly more fruitful if books can be used and religious language introduced into an already rich vocabulary, so that learners can reflect and come to their own conclusions in an articulate way. Though the church has in the past successfully preached the gospel to unlettered peoples, missionaries soon proceeded to translate the Scriptures and service books; draw up dictionaries and grammars for languages and dialects not previously reduced to writing; and then set up schools to teach literacy to new converts. But in our society today, the kind of Learning and Exploration needed can hardly begin without the use of books, captions and speech on TV and films, CD ROMS etc. And all require verbal proficiency.

The second Background Condition is *Autonomy*[11] (or 'normal' autonomy).[12] This in our discussion is the ability to make a rational choice in a controversial area. Autonomy involves thinking for oneself and being able to think well, to reflect rationally by the canons of thought in the various disciplines of learning. Also needed is the wider requirement of being able to judge for oneself, to come to a verdict and to follow it through into action and living. The autonomous person is able to resist the pressures of peers, parents, prejudice, tradition and early training. People from backgrounds unsympathetic to religion or religious in ways not easily open to new thinking will not be capable of learning and exploration, even if they have the verbal ability and motivation, unless autonomous to an high degree. Exploration in the realm of religious belief by its very nature presupposes an autonomous explorer, as does Commitment. For one cannot commit oneself except by personal choice. Now autonomy is not natural in many cultures, including our own and needs cultivating. So *Autonomy* is our second Background Condition for religious communication.

Our third Background Condition is *Opportunity* to learn and to explore. For communication takes time and effort. Pupils attend school or college, adults will need to be present at church or some equivalent. The evangelist and the potential convert must meet for a period. The Communicatee must be able to offer time, relatively free from distraction, worry or other matters. Even to read a book or to watch a film or video with attention needs leisure and concentration. The Communicatee also requires inner, psychological space, free from pressure to remain in a particular lifestyle from which he or she may wish to change.

All kinds of pressures, hindrances and stress in real life mean that opportunity to stand back, to think and to change is not always available. So we make this our third Background Condition. It becomes a matter to which the Communicator needs to give conscious attention and for want of which his or her attempts often fail or never even begin, because there is no chance for the processes denoted by our first Five-Stage Model to take place.

Whatever the faith to be communicated, and at all our stages in the communicative enterprise, these Background Conditions need to obtain. Unlike our Stages, which are necessary conditions of the next Stage occurring, the Background Conditions are necessary for any one or more of the later Stages. So we need to add *Verbal Ability, Autonomy* and *Opportunity* to our first Five-Stage Model for our statement of our General Theory of Religious Communication to be complete.

(iv) The Second, the Communicator's Model

Our discussion so far has focussed on what religious communication demands of the subject, the Communicatee, and the various stages he or she needs to undergo and the background conditions that must first be satisfied. But it is also important to look at the process from the other end, from the viewpoint of the Communicator, as well as from that of the Communicatee. When the enterprise is seen from the Communicator's standpoint, it becomes possible to simplify the presentation of the theory by presenting the Background Conditions as earlier, extra stages and to convert it into a series of tasks that Communicators must undertake or of steps they must take. In particular the Background Conditions can now be thought of as matters the agent must try to secure, before undertaking any one or more of the tasks that constitute the five stages of the First Model.

Thus we derive our Second Eight-Stage Model. The theory is now set out as eight steps or an eightfold path the Communicator must cause the Communicatee to travel along. Here we reach the final form of the Theory and the form to be mainly used in our further exposition and discussion. The Eight Stages or Steps are as follows:

I Verbal Ability
II Autonomy
III Opportunity
IV Nourishing the Sense of God
V Motivation
VI Learning
VII Exploration
VIII Commitment

(These names of Stages are hereafter printed in *italics* and begin with Capitals.)

In this Chapter we derived our first Five-Stage Model by adding a new stage to the earlier Four-Stage one we devised to clarify the task of Religious Education. Then we placed three Background Conditions which have to hold before and during the first stages of religious communication. Finally we shifted our stance to the Communicator's viewpoint and gave him or her an eightfold task, thus producing our Second Eight-Stage Model of a General Theory of Religious Communication.

Notes

[1] v. **1** (6)
[2] Mitchell, B. (1973), *The Justification of Religious Belief*, Macmillan, London, **5;** (1994), op. cit., **1–5.**
[3] Festinger, L. (1957), *A Theory of Cognitive Dissonance*, Stanford University Press,California,**1, 11** esp. 16–17.
[4] Newbigin, L. (1983), op. cit., 22ff., 32–60; (1986), op. cit., 31ff.; (1989), op. cit., 7, 215–233; (1991), op. cit., 55f.
[5] Francis, L. (1996), **14**, in Astley, J. and Francis, L. J. Eds., *Christian Theology and Religious Education* , S.P.C.K., London; Kay, W. K., Francis, L. J. and Gibson, HM(1996), Attitude to Christianity and the Transition to Formal Operational Thinking, *British Journal of Religious Education*, **19. 1**, 36.
[6] Brierley, P., op. cit. ,maintains 27% of the population are Secular, Atheist, Agnostic; cf. Gill R., op. cit., 203–207; Davie, G., op. cit., 77–87.

[7] We use this phrase 'Sense of God' in something like Bowker, J's sense. Cf. his (1973), *The Sense of God: Sociological, Anthropological & Psychological Approaches to the Sense of God*, O. U. P.; and (1978), *The Religious Imagination and the Sense of God*, O. U. P. Bowker's concern is the origin and explanation of the Sense of God: ours is how to nourish it in secular people.

[8] Fowler, op.cit.; Kohlberg, L. (1981), *Essays in Moral Development*, vol.1, Harper Row, London.

[9] Dearden, R. (1968), *The Philosophy of Primary Education*, Routledge and Kegan Paul, London , 121.

[10] Mitchell (1994), op. cit., 147.

[11] Astley, J. (1994), *The Philosophy of Christian Religious Education*, R.E.P., Birmingham, Alabama, 204–208; Norman, R. (1994), 'I did it my way.' Some Thoughts on Autonomy, *Journal of the Philosophy of Education*, **28:1,** 25–34.

[12] Thiessen, op. cit., 124–134 for valuable qualification of the degree of autonomy it is reasonable to promote in education ('normal' autonomy), in the light of recent criticisms of absolute autonomy. Cf. Also Haworth, L. (1986), *Autonomy*, Yale University Press, Newhaven and London for a valuable analysis of the growth of autonomy as a natural ability in human beings, but an analysis more concerned with action than with belief.

Chapter 4

Background Conditions

In this Chapter we expand on the treatment in Chapter III of our three Background Conditions of *Verbal Ability, Autonomy and Opportunity* in our first 5-Stage Model, (the Communicatee's Model), which are also the first three stages in the second 8-Stage Model of our Theory, (the Communicator's Model). In each case we explain how the presence or absence of the Condition concerned may be diagnosed. Further, we discuss how in general terms the Communicatees, particularly children, can be provided with what is lacking or how existing provision for this lack can be identified. Our constituency will be members of churches or other religious communities, including children, and the public at large, to all of whom they wish to communicate the faith.

(i) Verbal Ability

First we need to distinguish literacy, the ability to read and comprehend a text, from oracy, the ability to speak, to give talks, to listen with understanding and to share in discussion. Verbal ability covers both these competencies.

Strictly speaking, literacy in itself is dispensable for religious communication, although in practice it is very hard to dispense with. Obviously communication can begin with young children, who cannot read, but as children grow up into adults, literacy becomes more and more important. So we shall assume it is normally required in our advanced, secular and modern society. Also remember that in education, literacy is developed hand in hand with oracy.

It is also hard to say what level of literacy is needed for our Theory. Clearly the level will not be so high as that demanded for A-Level or degree study in the main disciplines. Therefore our theory is not elitist. Thus while one can be sure a graduate is literate enough, so of course is a person who has the conventional 5 GCSEs at Grades A to C, or other comparable school-leaving qualifications. Perhaps equally we may suspect the absence of sufficient literacy in a school-leaver without any academic qualifications; and look for an equivalent competence at reading in other countries.

Since in most advanced countries, with the kind of secular, plural culture we are concerned with, universal schooling is compulsory, sufficient literacy in our Communicatees ought to be able to be taken for granted. For soon after children can speak, they are supposed to learn to read and write and to develop their linguistic powers. Of course it does not follow that, because they can read in the technical sense, that they can 'bark at print' or decode written language, they understand the text and are fluent, able and willing to discuss it. Passing the Key Stage 1 and 2 in the National Curriculum[1] or perhaps reaching the expected Level 4 in SATS[2] (official tests in British schools), will give the level of literacy we look for in our *Verbal Ability* condition.

One gets the impression in Urban Priority Area(UPA) parishes and areas of social deprivation that the degree of literacy found is often poor[3] with a striking gender difference.[4] Men are worse at reading than women, and find expressing themselves in words difficult. In this simple fact may be found some part of the explanation of why men are so much less prone to attend church and to be active committed church-members than women. It might indeed be that in some age-groups and social strata, such as 6th Forms and Student populations, gender differences in personality orientation (as found by Francis and Wilcox)[5] could explain differences in religious behaviour and attitude. Otherwise men may well be hindered in being able to respond to our species of Communication by difficulties in oracy and literacy.

Such weaknesses may stand in the way of effective *Learning* and *Exploration*, however motivated these Communicatees are. The *Evangelist* or *Nurturer*, whether of children or adults, cannot really get started with those who find a verbal message hard to comprehend. Men who cannot express themselves in words will not be able to join with real competence in *Inter-Faith Dialogue*, an essentially linguistic exercise. And they will lack the educational qualification needed for the *Academic Study of Religion* or for serving the church professionally – this requires some ability to speak, read, write and discuss, which are central in *Ministerial Formation*.

Even if further research finds that lack of *Verbal Ability* is not a material factor in the differential response given to religious communication by gender, a parallel argument to that just given can be developed. Whatever turns out to be the major explanatory variable will indirectly impede successful religious communication and so will presumably account for the relative failure of the normal and special attempts by churches to reach men.[6] And steps will have to be taken to enable males to be in a fair and not disadvantaged position to learn about and to explore faith. *'Verbal Ability'* will have to be broadened to cover whatever is wanted to prepare the way for autonomy, so that whatever compensatory training is needed can be given to boys early in their lives. For example, if females have greater susceptibility to guilt feelings,[7] it might be possible to alter the socialisation of young boys so they grow up more sensitive to inner feelings of moral failure.

In deprived areas of city and country we find both sexes are reluctant to write letters, even when they need to: so one aspect of literacy is deficient. Many homes will have few books, yet the church expects them to cope with Bible, Service Books and Hymn Books! Thus the other side of literacy also falls short. To meet this difficulty one approach sometimes tried is to simplify liturgy and avoid the use of books as far as possible in religious communication. It is hard to believe, however, that much *Evangelism, Nurture, Inter-Faith Dialogue, Religious Education* or *Child Nurture* can get very far without books, still less the Academic *Study of Religion* or *Ministerial Formation*. It may be alleged that many adults learn about their hobbies from books and so could tackle religious books, if suitably motivated. We doubt, however, whether the people we refer to here, who lack basic literacy, can study their hobbies in books. The adults who can profitably use works in the fields of their own special interests will be those who have attained the minimum literacy also needed for religious communication. And even if books can be done without, oral discussion involving fluency and comprehension cannot. It is preferable therefore to hope that with better education all will one day become mature readers and will have the literacy and oracy sufficient for our purposes.

If we ask how Communicators may secure the *Verbal Ability* they need, we see they have to rely on a good home background and on good general education. Where such a background is lacking, education will have to compensate for this in developing *Verbal Ability*. This is one reason why the church and other religious communities should support schools and the work of teachers, especially with boys, and why in particular churches should keep denominational schools and a share in teacher training and ensure a religious presence on governing bodies. It should be noted in this connection that, in respect of *Verbal Ability, Religious Education* presupposes general education. To promote the beginnings of literacy and oracy is part of the case for pre-school education in the form of nursery schools, playgroups or pre-schools. When toddlers spill paint, sand, glue or water on the church hall floor, church authorities should remember that by being tolerant, they are encouraging language development and thus helping to satisfy the first *Background Condition* of Religious Communication.[8]

With existing young people and adults, whose verbal ability is poor, instead of simplifying texts and making the church user-friendly to the illiterate and inarticulate – which should also be done – support needs to be given to basic literacy courses in adult education, in prison education and in training schemes for the unemployed. In the youth service, in any kind of employment training or industrial chaplaincy activity, discussion generating oracy and comprehension of ideas should be encouraged. In a vast diversity of ways, the Communicator may thus help the first *Background Condition* to be satisfied, by concentrating on the first Stage, creating *Verbal Ability*.

(ii) Autonomy

Autonomy or normal autonomy is best approached negatively, by way of discussing how to counter the obstacles to young people and adults being capable of thinking, of choosing for themselves and then of committing themselves, which religious communication requires. And it should be noted that autonomy is not a trait to be expected in children before mid or late adolescence.

We should first note that *Autonomy* presupposes *Verbal Ability*, for how otherwise can people think for themselves or formulate the choices they face and debate them, except in language? This is why *Autonomy* follows *Verbal Ability* as our Second Background Condition or Stage.

Autonomy also involves being able to withstand various pressures to conform. In *The Lonely Crowd* and *Individualism Reconsidered*,[9] David Riesman distinguishes the 'autonomous' (or 'self-directed') person from the 'tradition-directed', the 'inner-directed', and the 'other-directed'. The 'tradition-directed' follows unselfconsciously the rules, customs and practices handed down in their community. The 'inner-directed' has his or her values set firm in early childhood, like having a gyroscope spinning inside. The 'other-directed' conforms to whatever are the norms in the surrounding peer group or current fashion, having sensitive radar antennae to keep him or her attuned to the signals of others.[10] Here again it is general education that should help a pupil to counter these pressures, though it is perhaps unclear how far in fact schooling promotes autonomy or vice versa. For if a student is successful in education, it may mean he or she can resist the pressures of early training, of the tradition in which they stand and of their peers. In Fowler's faith-development theory, autonomy only arrives at Stage IV. Children's and adults' faith at Stages I to III lack autonomy as one of its salient characteristics.[11] So of course, much religious communication will take place before autonomy is achieved. Many facts and skills can be learnt without this *Background Condition* obtaining.

Now young people will not, however, be able to proceed to *Exploration* and *Commitment* in any real sense, unless and until autonomy is developed as they grow into maturity. And once autonomy is attained, Communicatees who have come to accept the claims of a religion will then be able to exercise their ability to commit themselves to a faith, since to have this ability is a key element in autonomy that people today so often lack. Obstacles to autonomy emerging may well lie in the home, the social milieu, the peer group or the media.

One particular cause of autonomy being blocked in early childhood is the 'inner-directedness' of gender-differentiated personality formation.[12] Boys are socialised into those masculine qualities that prejudice men against religion. The properties they are proud to excel in are just those that faith, at least in its Christian form, is perceived to lack and so they cannot take it seriously and examine its claims dispassionately. Young men need to be brought up to be more feminine, without being any the less masculine, so that the effect of stereotypical male prejudice can be lessened and a greater possibility allowed of being 'self-directed' rather than 'inner-directed'.

It follows that a general upbringing for normal autonomy cannot be identical for boys and girls. Special obstacles to autonomy in males may require extra countermeasures. And by a similar argument, particular procedures of education and training may need to be applied to selected groups of children, so as to compensate for tendencies in some environments to result in young people growing up to be so 'tradition-directed' or 'peer-directed', that they cannot learn or explore religion effectively. In some cultures the Christian (or other) Communicator may have to undertake a correction to child-development, in order to modify ethnic or even religious socialisation that prevents autonomy, however hard this may be in practice.

Such special procedures will be additional to the general encouragement for 'self-direction' that this *Stage* of *Autonomy* requires. Youth work, pastoral care, chaplaincy in hospital or jail or college or factory, will all contribute to easing children's passage into autonomy as they travel through their teens. Also in similar ways this attribute may be strengthened in mature adults. Once again the Religious Communicator will support all these endeavours. With children he or she will encourage a style of child-rearing that gives both a firm base in a young life of order and security and later, on this foundation, autonomy as the capability to launch out into spiritual exploration.[13] Moreover in adolescence sticking to decisions reached will have to be insisted on so a young person learns what it is to commit oneself to what has been autonomously chosen.

Our concern in Religious Communication is not only autonomy but rational autonomy,[14] the ability of Communicatees to think for themselves competently. Again what is needed is a good general education in the various curricular disciplines, not merely the imparting of background information but the inspiring of a propensity to operate rationally with the concepts and criteria of each subject.[15] In England we shall hopefully be able to rely upon the National Curriculum, the Cross-Curricular Themes,[16] Personal and Social Education(PSE) and Citizenship, in particular, to nourish rational autonomy. We include the moral education of pupils which will figure as a prominent element in the later Stages of our Theory, which itself will foster autonomy. It can be developed as part of, a condition or consequence of all these enterprises and they cannot go far without it.

Autonomy is the *Background Condition* needed for *Exploration* and *Commitment*, a mind-set prepared for in childhood but only later to emerge in adulthood as a critical spirit. It is indeed possible, however, that later in life *Autonomy* might be nurtured and become real. But there will be no point in creating *Verbal Ability*, in providing *Opportunity* and *Motivation* for *Learning* unless a person, by the time they have begun to pass through these Stages has the freedom to explore and to bring to bear upon religion his or her rational mind.

It is not easy to describe the degree or level of *Autonomy* required for our Theory and it is hard to know how to recognise it. General attainment in education may be a rough guide, as with *Verbal Ability*, yet many well-educated adults are not truly autonomous. The proof of the pudding in this case may well be in the eating: can the Communicatee explore effectively without stress and anxiety? If he or she does lack independence of mind, maybe even then it is not too late to generate autonomy by practising discussion on non-controversial matters. By disputing issues that are not too difficult, emotive or existential, autonomy may be produced in discussion when the conclusions that emerge are not seen as threatening or disturbing and when pastoral support may build up confidence. Though a minimal measure of *Autonomy* has not been developed much earlier in life, the Communicatee may be able to face issues fairly, honestly and freely enough for *Exploration* to be possible and worthwhile.

(iii) Opportunity

When the Communicator wants to offer chances of being taught or of *Learning* in other ways, occasions of *Exploring* and/or considering *Commitment*, he or she first needs to study the Communicatee's life to see whether appropriate opportunities exist or can be provided. It is a matter for common sense judgement in relation to prior aims and the kind of communication envisaged.

Compulsory attendance at school, for instance, gives time and *Opportunity* for Religious Education; chaplains in prisons and hospitals may have similar opportunities not just to do pastoral work but to teach staff, prisoners and patients. No religious motivation is needed to make pupils attend school or prisoners or patients to be available. Otherwise strong and sustained interest is required for people to arrange opportunities, or to take advantage of chances for religious *Learning* or *Exploration* that are offered to them. Frequently the Communicator will have to intervene so that the Background Condition of providing *Opportunity* is satisfied on a day and at an hour to suit the Communicatee. Distance-learning and domiciliary tuition are examples of practice appropriate to modern conditions.

The Communicator will moreover need to explore which periods of a person's life today offer enough leisure for Religious Communication. In the First Age, as it is termed, the school-child may have no time for other commitments outside the classroom; students in higher education today, perhaps more under pressure than their predecessors, may still have more leisure than those in the next stage of life. The Second Age of full time employment (except for the unemployed) and caring for children may, in the modern world, allow little scope for Religious Communication. However it is the Third Age today that lasts so long and will offer to many the *Opportunity* needed: in retirement the pressures are off and the third Background Condition is satisfied.

In our society, sadly, the poor and deprived live under such daily pressures and stresses as to leave no freedom to learn, explore, to stand back and to view life steadily and to view it whole, which is a precondition of Religious Communication. Similarly it may well be that ill-health, the stress and suffering of bereavement, divorce, homelessness, change of job or residence cause people to be short of leisure and deprive them of the inner space needed to receive the communication of faith. Paradoxically, though, some argue that various kinds of disturbing transitions in living make people more open to new ideas and break up the hard ground of prejudice, habit and complacency.[17] To provide *Opportunity* in these conditions demands creative imagination of the Communicator.

At this point a serious objection to our argument needs considering. It might have been thought better to have located the Stage of providing *Opportunity*, since it will consist of making arrangements, just prior to actual classes or courses or meetings, which operationalise our Stages of *Learning* and *Exploration*. We call providing *Opportunity* a *'Background'* condition, though, precisely because Communication cannot *begin* until the Communicatees know they have a real chance to learn and explore. In fact we place *Opportunity* where it is in our sequence because the other *Background Conditions* of *Verbal Ability* and *Autonomy* should be satisfied by the normal social processes of upbringing and education. There is, of course, no problem in providing opportunity for these. The actual practical steps which have to be taken by the Communicator are indeed geared to make *Learning, Exploration* and possibly *Commitment* possible. So it could be said that making *Opportunity* should underpin these later stages in our scheme.

Opportunity is, however, placed before *Motivation* and its presupposition of *Nourishing the Sense of God*, since it will be hard to excite interest in a new and maybe strange field (religion!) if the subject sees no realistic prospect of being able to take up, follow through or act upon this interest. The two Stage sequence to generate the curiosity and concern the Communicatee requires are best left together, since they are jointly needed to generate present and lasting interest in matters to do with God. Hence providing *Opportunity* is introduced here, as our third Background Condition, since such conditions, we have said, are necessary not only to the immediate, next following Stage, but to any one or more of the succeeding Stages.

Thus it is that before Christian or other Religious Communication can really get under way, *Verbal Ability, Autonomy* and *Opportunity* need satisfying, wherever it may chance in a person's life that *Learning* etc. can be undertaken. Hence the *Background Conditions* of our first Model, (the Communicatee's Model), are placed before the stadial sequence opens. But in the second Model, when we set out by contrast the Communicator's programme, these *Background Conditions* become stages placed at the beginning of the analysis of what is required and what will in practice often be his or her earliest concern. Once then these *Background Conditions* are satisfied, *Motivation* and what prepares for it can begin to be considered.

Notes

1. Department for Education (1995), H. M. S. O., London.
2. Ibid., 26 ff.
3. Bynner, J. and Steedman, J. (1995), *Difficulties with Basic Skills*, The Basic Skills Agency, London, **1**. (It is interesting that this study of 21year olds in 1991 did not find an appreciable sex difference.) Ekinsmyth, C. and Bynner, J., *The Basic Skills of Young Adults*, The Basic Skills Agency, London, **2,4**.
4. v. **2** (25).
5. v.**2** (iv).
6. v. **2** (iii).
7. Argyle and Beit-Hallahmi, op. cit., *77,* 195–196.
8. v. **2** (iii).
9. (1950),Yale University Press, Newhaven; (1954), Free Press of Glencoe, New York.
10. (1950), op. cit.; (1954), op. cit., **II 2, III 9.**
11. Astley, J. and Francis, L. J. Eds. (1992), *Christian Perspectives on Faith Development*, Gracewing, Leominster.
12. iv **2**.
13. Thiessen, op. cit., 140-143 and references therein; Levinson, M. (1999), *the demands of liberal education,* O. U. P. , Oxford, 22–35.
14. Norman, R., op. cit., 25–34, esp. 29 ff.
15. Hirst, P. H. (1974), Liberal Education and the Nature of Knowledge in *Knowledge and the Curriculum*, Routledge and Kegan Paul, London, **3,4,6**.
16. or "Whole School Issues"(as they are now known). National Curriculum Council, *The Whole Curriculum*, Curriculum Guidance No.3.
17. Spriggs, D. (1995), Transition Times, *Church Growth Digest*, Moggerhanger Park, **16. 3**, 3–4.

Chapter 5

Nourishing the Sense of God

In this chapter we describe the first phase in motivating people to take an interest in western and other theistic religion.[1] Before we reach the *Stage of Motivation* proper, we come to *Nourishing the Sense of God*,[2] Stage IV in our Theory. We explain what is meant by our term 'the Sense of God'; discuss how it may be nourished; and suggest how to recognise when the Communicatee has sufficient intensity in his or her Sense of God for motivation to be possible for religious *Learning* and *Exploration*.

(i) The Sense of God

Interest is best generated in a field with which Communicatees are familiar and involved and which contains things of importance to them. In our secular age, ex hypothesi, people do not have familiarity or involvement with religion. So in order to become interested in theistic religion, we require that this dimension of experience is made familiar and a matter of concern. This spiritual dimension in which the whole of life and existence is related to a theistic focus is what is distinctive of a (mainly) western faith (and Sikhism): in a similar way religious beliefs and claims may be identified as those which lead back directly or indirectly to God.

What is required then in the Communicatee, at the outset, is at least a minimal belief that God exists. For atheists and agnostics, as soon as they have lost belief in God, not surprisingly lose interest in a faith directed towards the deity (except perhaps in academic or historical questions of philosophy or theology). A living religion depends on belief that God exists. Now the evidence is that most people in our society today do have such a minimal theistic belief.[3] Maybe this is partly because their belief is thin and vague and makes no personal demands. (If their belief were to challenge them profoundly in an existential way, they might then examine their belief critically and reject it. An indirect effect of enriching and deepening their superficial belief might well be to produce unbelief and then an apologetic for theism would be needed.)

Thus this thin and vague belief of a Communicatee is our starting-point but it cannot be left as it is. Such a nebulous popular theism will not bear the weight put upon it. Mere faith in God's existence needs deepening and intensifying. There are two elements in this process, which will produce what we shall call below a Sense of God.

First an adequate concept of God must be conveyed. God is not a non-personal force or field but a bodiless agent, creator of the world, who can change things, the living God of the Bible, not just an absentee landlord kind of 'ordinary god'.[4] Also by definition God is to be loved and served, worshipped and obeyed beyond all other claimants on our time, energies and life. He is our object of 'ultimate concern'.[5] The Communicatees have to grasp what would be for them the challenge of *believing* in God: if they were to believe in God, he would be their personal Lord and King, as contrasted with merely believing that some nebulous sort of God exists.[6]

The second element in having a Sense of God, which is implied by the idea of his being of ultimate concern to us, is that God is important and his claims upon us matter more than anything else in our lives, if we do grant his existence. To take on this existential theism with its idea of God's overwhelming significance for us is what really distinguishes the religious believer from the secular person, and it is this distinction which chiefly needs grasping by the Communicatee.

What kind of theism will the Communicator find in the Communicatee, as the enterprise of *Nourishing the Sense of God* begins? Many people have experiences of God[7] but we cannot take this experience for granted; widespread as such awareness is, it cannot be assumed in our communicative process, though where religious experience is found in Communicatees, the Communicator will rejoice and build upon it. Indeed if any of our Species of Communication is to get off the ground and make progress, more than a bare, non-personal, theoretical theism is needed (though less than an actual mystical, psychic or spiritual experience is necessary.) It may also be sufficient that a theist already has a Sense of God, though without ever having had any religious experience.

In cases, however, where the Communicatee is an unbeliever or a nominal believer only, what matters is to implant an adequate concept of God and a belief in the importance of the theistic focus in the life of worshippers. When this Sense of God is found, the Communicatee will be able to take the question of God's existence seriously. He or she may eventually believe that God exists or may not believe, as the case may be, but if they do believe, they will have real faith because their Sense of God has been sufficiently nourished. So what as a matter of psychological fact is required to be generated in the Communicatee at this Stage in our sequence is the possession of an adequate concept of the divine, plus the associated value judgement of the importance of the religious dimension: and this we term having a *Sense of God*. To have such an awareness is what is essential if a person is to be open to being motivated to learn and explore in the sphere of religion.

(ii) Nourishing the Sense of God

How may a sense of God be implanted in the majority who lack it? There are three main ways.

> (a) The first is through Religious Education in schools. Unless pupils grasp this categorial concept of the great theistic faiths,[8] they will not get far in understanding and exploring religious belief and its implications for living. Fortunately current Religious Education requires that the concept of deity in Christianity, Islam, Judaism, Sikhism and in some traditions within Hinduism, must be presented, despite a diversity of names and other terminology for the divine. Children's ideas of a bearded, old man above the sky needs refining and enriching as the key notion in the vocabulary of worship and spirituality, or prayer and meditation. To introduce pupils to this central concept, they need a combination of instruction and discussion, suited to the different ages and stages of schooling, with the actual use of term 'God' in worship-with-an- object[9] in Assembly and class prayers. To gain the idea of God, as one we can address and listen to, it is necessary for pupils in Assembly to go beyond the threshold of school worship into worship-with-an-object: also it is necessary that children transcend the mere celebration of common values and concerns that is coming to be the meaning of collective worship nowadays.[10]
>
> Since all children in Britain and in many other countries are compelled to attend school and to receive *Religious*

Education, the task of giving an adequate concept of God may now be assumed to be seriously attempted and its success dependent on that of Religious Education. (In the USA and other countries where there is no teaching of religion in the public or state schools, we have to count higher levels of churchgoing than in Britain as ways to equip people with a Sense of God). So the Sense of God will be first developed in childhood, but reinforcement in adulthood is obviously desirable.

(b) The second way to nourish the Sense of God is through adult worship. From time to time the Communicatee will attend and observe worship and learn how to address a personal deity and may even join in. Such encounters should strengthen people's grasp of the concept and bring the Communicatees to realise how important it is to worship, whether or not they themselves *do* believe in God.

Our Communicatee will meet worship in diverse ways. Adults who are non-practising Christians may only experience worship at Baptisms, Weddings, Funerals, Harvest Festivals, Mothering Sunday and other public occasions. But over a life time the cumulative effect of this acquaintance with prayer and praise should have a significant impact. Practising Christians (and members of other faiths), children or grown-up, should have their Sense of God nurtured by regular presence at religious services, in preparation for *Evangelism, Nurture* or *Inter-Faith Dialogue*. (For *Inter-Faith Dialogue*, it may be assumed that the non-Christian Dialogist has sufficient *Sense of God* from the mere fact that he or she is willing and able to enter into this activity.) In *Academic Study of Religion* and *Ministerial Formation*, it will be later argued,[11] the Stages of *Nurturing the Sense of God* and of *Motivation* will be unnecessary because we should be able to take for granted the motivation of students. However, it may be observed that people are unlikely to become students of Religious Studies or Theology or candidates for *Ministerial Formation*, if their interest has not been aroused earlier in life by encountering the worshipping community.

It is with the communicative activity of *Religious Education* that the biggest problem lies. In church schools pupils will encounter believing and practising teachers, parents, governors and a local church all co-operating to nourish faith and to make worshipping God something real and relevant. But children in county schools, who have no religious background at home or in a spiritual community, are the big problem. It is to be hoped that relevant and attractive school worship-with-an-object, especially in the Primary Phase where natural curiosity can be harnessed, may make some contribution to *Nourishing* the pupils' *Sense of God*. Failing that, Religious Education itself becomes problematic.

(c) The third means of *Nourishing the Sense of God* is through the witness of believers, both Christians and those of other theistic faiths. The witness needed is of four varieties.

First, Christians and others must lead loving and attractive lives and strive for social justice. To do this is good per se but it is also a condition of effective and plausible witness of the subsequent varieties to the non-practising and other non-members of the religions that focus on God. The believers' credibility is thus established.

The second kind of witness of the religious person is to the particular values and practices that distinguish the faithful from the majority in a secular age. The chief of these is worship; others may lie in the area of sexual ethics. To attend church and to honour marriage speak loudly of what is held sacred. To practise these is a living exhibition of what it is to take God seriously. Without this kind of witness religion is not distinctive; without the first kind it is not compelling. Together they are enough to win respect but not enough to arouse interest or to pave the way for further communication.

The third kind of witness is to say a word in season about belief in God. Unless heralded by witness of the first two sorts, witness in word will not be heeded. But following on from them, explanation and argument, simple and ad hoc or extended and systematic, can help *Nourish the Sense of God* by supporting the claim that the Communicatee is by now beginning to suspect may be true, the astounding hypothesis that the weighty concept of God may actually have something in existence corresponding to it – in short that God is real.

Those whose witness is of the first three kinds, by their personality, values and words, by all they are, may also show that God is real to them. And this is the fourth kind of witness. An English officer, in the last days of the war, in a concentration camp, said of Bonhoeffer that he had never met a man whose God was so real to him.[12] This type of witness is closely connected psychologically with spirituality. When a person is in close, regular, frequent and intimate contact with God by prayer, they will become transparent to God, a window into the divine, without words or deeds being necessary to their religious identity. Such in our day was Archbishop Michael Ramsay.[13] From the fact that these people live close to God and that He is of supreme importance to them, the Communicatees will also come to sense that that God should be central in their lives.

Thus simply by manifesting all four kinds of witness, many people can act as Communicators in *Nourishing* someone's *Sense of God*. Needless to say it behoves the church (and other faith-communities) to train their practising and committed members in witness of these four kinds, just as the nurturing power of worship can be fostered by making it clear, lively, enjoyable and exciting.

(d) A fourth way that may be able to strengthen and deepen a person's *Sense of God*, and make vivid their belief that he exists, (if they do hold such a belief), is through reflection on the contingency of things. This approach will only be possible, however, for those who wish to have their *Sense of God nourished* and who are willing to undertake the meditation required. This is unlikely to be the case with *Evangelism* (and superfluous in the case of *Inter-Faith Dialogue* with the devout of other religions) where, ex hypothesi, people are uninterested and will probably be unwilling to indulge in a time-consuming exercise: the whole point of this Stage in *Evangelism* is to operate on the Communicatee from outside, without their positive co-operation, so that they will be rendered open to being motivated later. But the consent of the Communicatee is more likely to be given in adult *Nurture;* children will usually respond positively to the Communicator in *Child Nurture;* in *Religious Education,* the *Academic Study of Religion* and *Ministerial Formation*, the teacher can properly offer this imaginative technique for gaining a more intense awareness of God as an exercise in empathy with believers, showing what it is like to take God seriously.

The meditative approach needed for deepening the Communicatee's Sense of God begins by getting him or her to realise their own transience: reflect on the fact that once I did not exist and one day I shall exist no longer; contemplate the graves of the long-departed who once were alive as I am now and yet are gone! Then compare yourself with an ancient building, rock or mountain. These appear immovable, unchangeable and indestructible, while our human life-span by contrast is so very brief. But remember old piles of stone do not last for ever. Not even the world is eternal. It began with the Big Bang and may end with the Big Crunch!

Such reflections give one a sense of radical contingency: since I (and the rest) are so transient, I might well have never existed. Nothing might have come to be. Yet in fact I do exist, as do ancient edifices, stones and hills. How can this be unless there is behind everything an eternal Source of being, what we call God or the Creator. Things exist because he supports them and his existence explains theirs'. To practice such meditation over a period of time may strengthen and vivify the Communicatees' Sense of God, if they believe in God. In a mind stilled and emptied of distracting thoughts, God's reality may become a pressing conviction, not far from the awareness of God that some claim is a normal human experience[14] or perhaps an awareness generated by worship.[15]

This procedure, if successful, is not of course, it must be stressed, an *argument* for God's existence,[16] certainly not a rational appeal to religious experience, nor a substitute for natural theology. It is rather a self-induced deepening and intensifying of the conviction that God is real, important and of existential concern to everyone on the part of those who have this conviction.

(iii) Assessing Stage IV

How may we tell that someone has a sufficient Sense of God? This may be mainly decided by the Communicatee's openness to becoming interested in religion and by their being excited by the prospect of finding out more and searching further. In practice the Communicator will always be trying Stage V activities in the hope of motivating some individual or group of Communicatees he or she has in mind. Something sparks off an interest deep enough to move a person to want to learn or to explore, cognitive dissonance is clearly aroused. The Communicator must not drop his or her efforts but has to check whether the underlying Sense of God in the Communicatee(s) is deep enough and sincere enough to enable the fire of interest to go on burning and progress to be made. But if the fire is not yet lit, Stage IV is incomplete and any dissonance so caused is of too small a magnitude to be effective in generating motivation.

By its very nature this Stage is a protracted operation. *Nurturing* a person's *Sense of God* begins in childhood with *Religious Education*, if it does not begin in the home – as is all too rarely the case nowadays! Then a person has a lifelong, if erratic, exposure to worship, so long as he or she lives in a society where religions are active and worship occurs. In a secular age where, as was said above[17] the norm is to be profoundly uninterested in religious matters, it will be a great achievement so to *Nourish* people's *Sense of God* that their eyes are opened to the possibility of learning about and investigating the claims of God. Stage IV is thus the biggest challenge and task for the religious Communicator in a secular, plural society: it is to support, not logically but psychologically, Newbigin's claim that in our culture faith can be public truth, objective knowledge about the universe, like science, and not just a matter of subjectivity or of value judgement in the private sphere.[18]

One final difficulty should be noted. When people's Sense of God deepens and intensifies, as we saw above, they may become unbelievers in God now that they really understand how great the demands of faith are. Their theistic belief will collapse and crumble when they realise who God is and that he *matters*. Then comes the time for a fuller witness in words; in books, lectures, discussions, in *Religious Education* or in other settings. An apologetic for theism, a rational case for belief in the real God must be put forward.[19] But this means that Communication has in effect rapidly advanced, taking in the Stage of *Motivation,* expanding to *Learning* and to

Exploration of the rationale of theism. So real belief may replace conventional faith via first *Nourishing the Sense of God*, then provoking scepticism and finally renewing conviction that the Lord God exists and matters.

(iv) The Case for God's Reality

This study is about religious communication. We are not writing a full-blown work in the philosophy of religion and we have not the space to present here a comprehensive case for God's existence. Nonetheless it is desirable at this point to offer some brief account of how such an argument for God's reality might be framed today. Thus we indicate one crucial place for religious apologetic, the fuller witness in words just referred to above. In Section (iii) we showed this would be needed when people realise the great weight of God's claims and how they bear on us. Once this awareness dawns, as we have said, a Communicatee might well decide it is more prudent not to believe in God: atheism is a safer bet!

We are also able by this piece of apologetic to answer a question that may be provoked by our insistence on the importance of the Godward dimension of human existence. Unless there are grounds for holding that the concept of God is not empty and that there corresponds to it in reality an active, individual agent and creator of the world, why should the deity be thought significant and the *Sense of God* a thing to *nurture*? Is the generation of this conviction, however it may be achieved psychologically, a reasonable procedure?

Considerations showing the case for God to be reasonable and reasons that it is therefore proper to produce a sense of God's importance, also illustrate the use of philosophical argument in determining religious truth and hence provide one criterion for the truth of a particular faith or for that of inter-faith claims. Later in discussing the *Exploration* of religion as giving objective knowledge of the world, such a criterion will be invoked: at this present point in our discussion we can anticipate its employment and see how it operates.

We have already outlined theism as we conceive it and the concept of a personal transcendent God.[20] Our question now is, does any real being satisfy such a concept? In other words, does God exist? In the case we now give no originality is claimed. We present in summary form two arguments from recent work in the philosophy of religion by Markham and Swinburne.[21] Markham is chosen because of his originality as a younger philosopher of religion in grounding critical realism in a fusion of the cosmological and teleological arguments for theism; and Swinburne for a careful and thorough presentation of the argument from religious experience within a much wide account of natural theology. One of our approaches then to God's existence begins from objective truth; the other from religious experience.

Most people take for granted the possibility of objective truth in science, history and in common sense empirical matters. How the world is does not depend entirely on how we interpret and conceptualise it. Some kind of 'critical realism' is widely accepted today.[22] The only ultimate alternative is a thorough-going Nietzschean perspectivism and relativism.[23] But is such critical realism reasonable to accept if the world does not have a rational creator?

In so arguing we combine the old cosmological and teleological approaches. We ask why a world exists with an objective order, as discovered by science and other human knowledge, rather than nothing or chaos. It does not even seem reasonable just to assume such a world will stay in existence and remain open to profitable investigation from moment to moment. Why does the universe not dissolve into chaotic disorder next minute? Again why is the order science finds the same here as in distant galaxies, the same today as well as billions of light years ago?[24]

That the cosmos, so open to unlimited human investigation, is just accidental and inexplicable brute fact is simply incredible and outrages common sense. At this point argument can go no further and we just appeal to our basic belief that the world exists in an orderly fashion. Such a presumption may ultimately imply theism, as we think it does, even if most of those who have such a confidence in objective knowledge do not realise this. Our conviction, on which our case rests, is that this basic presupposition or 'faith', not obviously religious, is widespread in our culture among those with whom we wish to communicate.

What makes belief in an orderly world reasonable is belief in a personal creator, who is omnipotent, omniscient and omnipresent, who creates ex nihilo, in such a way that nothing can obstruct his originating and sustaining a universe. It is this creative process which is supportive of the objective knowledge discerned by a critical realism. The metaphysical character of such a creator is sketched by Markham[25] and fully set out by

Swinburne.[26] The essential point is to postulate such a creator with *'necessary being'*, which means he exists forever, and is indestructible and underived from any other being. Only the postulation of such a self-existent being can meet the requirement of answering the question why such a world as ours exists in fact, without raising the further question of why this creator himself exists. Thus we stop the apparent regress of gods behind God getting under way and the idea that God's own existence is only contingent and accidental as the ultimate source of order. The works referred to give plenty of extended argument to support and explicate this crucial consideration.[27]

The second argument for God's existence we deploy is from religious experience. Religious experience for our purposes is awareness of God, whether numinous and mystical *or* everyday and low-key, as opposed to usual sense-experiences (or unusual ones like ghosts) or, as in the case of a storm being God's anger, just the redescription of everyday perception of a tempest in terms of God's activity. The obvious contemporary objection that the object of religious experience is illusory can be answered by reference to various considerations. Empirical research shows that such experience does not mainly come to the poor and neurotic: thus this finding counts against the Marxist and Freudian explanations in terms of naturalistic assumptions as to how religion may arise.[28] A more fundamental point is that all experience of things is normally accepted at face-value, if human knowledge is ever to get off the ground. Swinburne calls this 'The Principle of Credulity':[29] when experience presents something as existent, as its object, we deem it reasonable to believe that the object of awareness does really exist, unless we have specific reason to the contrary.

Swinburne claims religious experience is not an exception to the Principle of Credulity.[30] There is no need to have additional evidence from the past to support the objective nature of religious experience, just as we do not need any such foundation for sense experience. While we properly conclude that what we see exists and causes our seeing of it, there is no need for a claim to apprehend God to require special backing. Experience of even past sensory experience cannot be used to support the present's objectivity without circularity; for in order to remember the past and to be correct in doing so, we already take for granted the Principle of Credulity, that memory is accepted at face value and the past is assumed to be reliable. Why should the same not be true of religious experience?

Nor can religious experience be fenced off, as a matter of an optional interpretation of basic data, while reserving to perception the claim to be accepted as objective as it stands. For many other claims to experience and to recognise things go beyond mere sensory experience. Mental states embodied in bodily configurations are not reducible to the product of bare observation, like looks, shapes and colours, and yet normally are taken to be perceived: the Principle of Credulity is indeed applied across the board. And so why not to religious experience?

Naturally within a religious tradition there will be criteria for distinguishing true from false apprehensions of God, Christ's voice from that of demons, or in contemporary terms genuine encounters with the divine from psychotic or other delusions. But these intra-religious discriminations are compatible with holding that the whole dimension of experience of God does indeed give evidence of God's existence, as much as ordinary sense experience does of physical objects.

Unless it can be shown that religious experiences can be produced to order by drugs or brain surgery or unless some other materialistic explanation can be produced, the Principle of Credulity works. No evidence at present exists to prove that apprehensions of God are mere products of such brain conditioning. Even if such proof could be found, it might only demonstrate the aetiology of religious hallucinations, like voices ordering crime, while leaving unimpaired the major part of worldwide experience of God. Indeed until there is conclusive philosophical argument produced to demonstrate that God does not or cannot exist, it is perfectly reasonable to believe that God, the real creator, uses mental mechanisms or brain processes to make himself evident to rational creatures in a material world.

Such are our two main arguments for God's existence. Presenting and evaluating them is, as we shall see,[31] how the Communicator or Communicatee applies the truth-criterion of philosophical reason to religious claims.

Before motivating people to learn and explore a religion's message, they have to have a real belief in a real God. Of course often there is no need to argue for such belief, but when belief in a personal Lord makes demands and challenges a person's whole way of life, just *Nourishing* their *Sense of God* may not be enough to preserve belief in God. In that case some apologia for theism, such as has been set out in this Section, can help. It does indeed appear that before learning about and exploring revelation or the distinctive positive teaching of one or other theistic faith, an old-fashioned natural religion in the eighteenth century sense of a pious attitude to a creator not known by special revelation in Scripture is required as a presupposition.

Communicatees will vary enormously in their level of sophistication at which an apologia has to be offered, from the level of philosophy of religion as a constituent of the *Academic Study of Religion* (and of *Ministerial Formation*) down to that of popular polemic in *Evangelism* and *Nurture* (of adults). Probably every good syllabus in *Religious Education* should include this element, just as courses in basic ethics or theodicy should be also covered. At some time or place good reasons for belief form part of the communicative process. The intellect needs convincing, as well as the imagination, head as well as heart, in *Nourishing* a person's *Sense of God* as a precondition of *Learning* and *Exploration*, so that the Communicatee has a vision of God as being a crucial to a good life. Such a person is now ready for *Motivation* and to this Stage in our Theory we now turn.

Notes

[1] v. 2 (ii)
[2] v. 2 (ii)
[3] Davies, op. cit. vii, 79 ff.
[4] Davies, op. cit., vii, 79.
[5] Tillich, P. (1947), *The Shaking of the Foundations,* SCM Press, London, 57.
[6] For believing in and believing that v. Price, H. H.(1964), Faith and Belief in Hick, J. Ed., *Faith and the Philosophers*, Macmillan, London, 3–25 esp. 8 ff.
[7] v. the work of the Alister Hardy Research Centre, Westminster College, Oxford, as in Hardy, A. (1979), *The Spiritual Nature of Man,* Clarendon Press, Oxford; and Hay, D. (1990), *Religious Experience Today*, Mowbray, London.
[8] v. Attfield, D. G. (1982), Conceptual Research in Religious Education, in Hull, J. Ed., *New Directions in Religious Education*, Falmer Press, Lewes, 77–84. Gaining the concept of a personal god is the more important in view of the long-term decline in this belief: v. Kay, W. K. *(1997),* Belief in God in Britain 1945–1996, *British Journal of Religious Education*, **20. 1**, 28–41.
[9] v. Attfield, D. G. (1996), Worship and Religious Education, *SPES* 4, 21–27 esp.21 ff.
[10] Ibid. 23ff
[11] 7(vi).

[12] Payne Best in The Venlo Incident, quoted in Bethge, E. Ed. (1953), *Dietrich Bonhoeffer, Letters and Papers from Prison*, (E. T.)Fuller, R. H., S. C. M. Press, London, 11.
[13] Chadwick, O. (1990), *Michael Ramsey,* O. U. P., Oxford, 361-362, 373-376.
[14] Lewis, H. D. (1959), *Our Experience of God*, Allen and Unwin, London, **1-3**.
[15] Astley, J. (1996), The Role of Worship in Christian Learning, 248-249, in Astley, J., Francis, L. J. and Crowder, C. Eds., *Theological Perspectives in Christian Formation*, Gracewing, Leominster.
[16] Cf. (v).
[17] v. **1** (iv), **2** (ii).
[18] v. **1** (20).
[19] e.g. Swinburne, R. (1979), *The Existence of God*, Clarendon Press, Oxford; Smart, J. J. C. and Haldane, J. J. (1996), *Atheism & Theism*, Blackwell, Oxford; Braine, D. (1988), *The Reality of Time and the Existence of God*, Clarendon Press, Oxford; Montefiore, H. (1985),*The Probability of God*, S. C. M. Press, London; Markham, I. (1998), *Truth and the Reality of God,* T. and T. Clark, Edinburgh.
[20] v. **5** (i).
[21] Markham, op. cit.; Swinburne, op. cit.
[22] Markham, op. cit., **3**; Hobson, P. R. and Edwards J. S. (1999), *Religious Education in a Pluralist Society,* Woburn Press, London, **4**.
[23] Markham, op. cit., **5**.
[24] Ibid., 80; Swinburne, op. cit., 136-151.
[25] Op. cit., 88-93.
[26] Op. cit., **6**; Swinburne, R. (1997), *The Coherence of Theism,* Clarendon Press, Oxford, **Pts. II** and **III**.
[27] Swinburne, (1977), op. cit.,**13 and 14**; (1979) op. cit., 92-93.
[28] Hay, op. cit.,86-89.
[29] Swinburne, (1979), op. cit., 254-255.
[30] Ibid.,255-260.
[31] v. **7** (iii).

Chapter 6

Motivation and Myers-Briggs

In this Chapter we consider how to motivate people so that they want to learn about religion, once their Sense of God has been aroused and intensified in Stage IV of our Theory of Religious Communication. Our approach is to suggest different areas in which interest may be stimulated for different sorts of person. For this purpose we introduce the 'Myers-Briggs typology',[1] its four polarities along which persons are divided and the four Character or Temperament types which emerge. We offer proposals for motivating each type; we analyse the task of the Communicator; and we describe the way in which this Stage of our Theory figures cumulatively in Religious Communication, in generating an interest to carry the Communicatee through all the subsequent Stages.

(i) The Myers-Briggs Typology

We have claimed that to motivate people for religious *Learning* and *Exploration*, interest has to be generated by instances of 'cognitive dissonance'.[2] These will occur between 'cognitive elements' – beliefs, attitudes and actions – within a field in which the Communicatee is personally involved and which he or she deems important. We have also seen that in a secular age the religious field is not normally one which persons are concerned with, unless or until this field is deliberately generated in them by the Communicator. Religious interest will arise only in persons whose *Sense of God* has been *nurtured* to a marked degree.[3] Now we can go on to analyse the kinds of stimulus, generating cognitive dissonance, which have to be placed in the Communicatees' theistic field, that has already been established by *Nourishing* his or her *Sense of God*.

Creative ingenuity may devise a myriad of stimuli of many kinds. In our discussion only a few suggestions of each kind will be made by way of illustration. But what we can usefully do is to propose that the kind of stimulus should systematically vary with the type of person to be motivated. It is a profound truism that people differ. Their energies flow in different directions; their perceptions are responded to at different levels of generality; conduct may be based on thought or feeling; some are task-orientated, others are driven by impulse and passing desire. These distinctions have been formulated in Jung's theory of personality types[4] and this affords a useful tool for Communicators to employ so that they approach Communicatees with stimuli that are appropriate and likely to be fruitful.

For our purposes then human differences are helpfully conceptualised in the Myers-Briggs typology.[5] This was devised by Isobel Briggs Myers, who developed Jung's famous distinctions and who operationalised them by creating an Instrument or test for classifying subjects, which is statistically reliable and valid and standarized on a large American population. Below we briefly summarise the main distinctions used; we concentrate on the positive qualities of each type and ignore the negative qualities that can give rise to personal deficiencies.

The first distinction of attitudes is between Extroverts(Es) and Introverts(Is).[6] This difference is by now so well known that it is part of modern common sense psychology. In Es energy mainly flows into the outer world of people and action. An E is happiest and least tired when interacting with others in all the busyness of social life. By contrast Is turn their energy inwards into the inner life of the mind and spirit and relate to figures and ideas and other elements within their hearts and minds.

The second distinction of attitude governs the way behaviour is regulated. People are polarised between Judgers(Js) and Perceivers(Ps).[7] Js give precedence to principles, plans, policies, projects and purposes. They are highly task- and goal-orientated. In their view time is short, energy scarce and ends beyond immediate desires override lesser concerns. Js hasten along the path of duty, looking neither to the right nor to the left, full of self-discipline, exhibiting the Puritan ethic of delayed gratification, concentrating on things to get done. By contrast Ps are casual and laid-back, unworried and unhastened by plan and policy, yielding to impulse and responding to what emerges as present desire, taking life as it comes, wandering off in ever new directions as they dawdle down the years.

Besides these two pairs of attitudes, Myers-Briggs also divides people into those dominated by two pairs of functions, one governing perception and one underlying action. The first pair of functions split mankind into Sensors(Ss) and Intuitionists(Ns).[8] Ss focus on minute particulars, on details, on what is present and immediate in life as it is experienced minute by minute. By contrast Ns select patterns from the flow of perception and respond at a more general level. They are happier with theories, full of imagination, lovers of diversity and of novel possibilities, more open to the future than tied down by the restrictive exigencies of the present.

The other pair of functions reveal two alternative bases for judgement. Behaviour must have explicit or implicit principles of action, and the considerations which dominate judgements fall into two groups, those characteristic of Thinkers(Ts) and those of Feelers(Fs).[9] For Ts intellect rules and reason guides and motivates conduct; whereas with Fs emotion sways the will as a person reacts to the world and acts within it.

By the Myers-Briggs Type Indicator an individual is placed at either end of these four polarities (two opposed attitudes, two pairs of functions). Four scores are used to divide the population, by taking every possible combination of results, into 16 personality types. It is as impossible as it is unnecessary for the religious Communicator to take account of the full range of such fine discriminations. We suggest an approach to motivation based first on the four functions and four attitudes (E/I, J/P, S/N, T/F). It is secondly also useful to consider four 'Character' or 'Temperament' types, which emerge from research as significant in studying possible pairs of functional or attitude differentiations and which seem to generate new characteristics not obvious from the basic polarities of the system. (The two basic functions S/N and T/F are wholly independent of one another and are the foundations for the four character types.)[10]

These four Characters or Temperaments are:-

NT 'Promethean', intellectual and imaginative, integrating ideas into systems, visionary, having a strong grasp of issues, enterprising, conscientious;

NF 'Apollean', sensitive and sympathetic, creative, seeking integrity and harmony, concerned about people and relationships;

SJ 'Epimethean', stable, conservative, practical and prepared, keen on order and tradition, loyal, supporting organisations and institutions, patient, responsible, carrying society's burdens;

SP 'Dionysian', trouble-shooting, impulsive, full of virtuosity, charm, flair and charisma, flexible and free, open-minded, talented, versatile, living fully in the present.

(ii) Motivation by Type and Temperament

It now becomes possible to suggest the kinds of stimulation appropriate for exciting interest in religious learning and exploration. In every case the Communicatee is brought into an external association with theistic religion, by whatever appeals to their type and character, prior to the later Stages of being informed, believing or committed. Cognitive dissonance will then arise between what faith stands for, by now of importance to the Communicatees, whose *Sense of God* has been *Nurtured,* and their personal lack of knowledge and interest in religion. So a pressure to reduce this dissonance and thus motivation to learn and to explore will result.

With the first pair of attitudes (Is and Es), it emerges that the right kind of situation for Es will be in the sphere of practical activity and social life for young and old. In a local church Es will flourish in organisations, like Youth Clubs and Senior Citizens Luncheon Clubs, doing manual work on buildings and grounds, and in concrete good works in the community as a part of the church's mission. They then feel 'cognitive dissonance' between what they are doing and the Godward dimension, which by now is important to them, yet which so far is unexplored and unknown; and thus there arises a pressure to learn and to explore.[11] But with Is the inner life of books, plays, drama, literature, discussion and spirituality will have more appeal and be a suitable context for dissonance.

The second pair of attitudes (Js and Ps) govern the timetable and programmes to be offered containing the dissonances required. For Js there can be courses of talks, lectures, sermons, like Alpha courses.[12] Books, which present topics in order, TV series, adult education syllabi will not cause strain nor deter or distract Js once they have put their hands to the plough. For Ps, impulsive and labile, courses or series would become burdensome; rather, a vast diversity in communicative programmes with many and varied one-off events will attract and enable them to latch on now to this and then to that stimulus, generating dissonance.

The first pair of functions are S and N. Ss will enthuse over detail – church decorations and furnishings, crafts, jobs to be done immediately – with a similar stimulating effect as with Es; or with introverted Ss, they will love to focus on the details of character and plot in stories, novels and narratives, in correct answers to quizzes, puzzles and crosswords. With Ns, however, the Gospel must be so presented as to appeal to the imagination: there is the sweep, scope and massive coherence of Christian doctrine, the great drama of the miracle plays from Creation to the Last Judgement, the vision of the Kingdom growing from the present situation to the end of history, the scale and magnificence of the major Masses, Passions and

Requiems in western music. Imaginative schemes to re-order churches and explore their message in architecture and art will be stimuli for Ns and present plenty of dissonance.

Finally there are the T and F functions to cater for. With Ts the Communicator will appeal to the intellect and concentrate on apologetics, rational exposition of belief and on reasons for faith in response to dissonance. But with Fs he or she will go for the heart rather than the mind, arousing sympathy, presenting vividly Jesus and his Passion, the lives of prophets and saints, pastoral concern, love for God and love for the human race; these are matters that stimulate search and enquiry, because these emotions are dissonant with the Communicatees' ignorance of and indifference to religion.

These sketchy contrasts in motivational approaches, orientated to the basic attitudes and functions in the Myers-Briggs typology, become clearer when the four Character and Temperament types are examined and addressed in terms of the stimuli and settings that will provide 'cognitive dissonance' and thus provoke interest.

NTs will respond to inspired preaching, lecturing and books that explore the great issues in philosophy and theology raised by the Christian faith in today's world. Plans and strategy for mission and reforming church structures, ethical and social problems in a secular age, the challenges to faith of science and technology, will appeal to NTs. If they are introverted it will be more the theoretical issues that will stimulate. Extroverted NTs e.g. pioneers, generals, architects, medical consultants, inventors, entrepreneurs, adventurers and engineers need to find the intersection of their professional concerns with the Gospel, as in the 'Gospel and Culture Movement'[13] or in the work of the Christian Frontier Council in an earlier age,[14] thus provoking the dissonance extrovert NTs will hopefully will feel between faith and their personal lack of it.

NFs will find stimulus in the more emotional side of the Gospel in liturgy and music, worship and drama: take them to the Passion play at Oberammagau or invite them to compose or produce their own drama in a local church. Alternatively hands on work for the aged, the disabled, refugees and prisoners of conscience will stimulate the dissonance required. For when the Communicatees work alongside Christians in Amnesty, Oxfam, Shelter (an housing charity) and suchlike bodies, endless opportunities to arouse interest in religion abound, provided the Communicatees' *Sense of God* has been well nourished.[15]

SJs will find their stimulus to learn about religion when they are invited to support the church as a traditional source of values, conserving the best of our national Christian past. Christianity may be presented as a force for stability and succour in our uncertain and perplexing age. At a simple level SJs may revel in the history of their parish church as a key element in the story of their neighbourhood. SJs will warm to the faith by being encouraged to take on positions of responsibility in the church as Wardens, PCC and Synod members and thus be open to *Nurture*: as teachers and especially head teachers in Church-schools, or in taking up practical responsibility in other voluntary bodies, provided the Christian inspiration of these organisations is made clear, SJs are potential learners and explorers. For then the desired dissonance, between the new practice and their existing weakness in faith, will motivate them to learn and explore.

Finally SPs, the fourth temperamental type, like prophets, are difficult to contain in the institutional church or in any other voluntary framework. But they may have energies and inspiration to become youth leaders, counsellors, adult educators, pioneers and innovators in the arts, drama and music, whether within the church or outside it. When such activity is combined with a well-*Nurtured Sense of God*, contact with Christians may cause sparks of interest to catch light and to burn brightly: dissonance will occur between their new interests and the Gospel, as a crucial but missing element in their personal outlook.

With every type of person and in connection with every activity, the quality of the friendship of the Christians, that the Communicatees have been brought into contact with, is an important factor in generating motivation. There is good empirical evidence that friendship is crucial in introducing newcomers to the church.[16] Indeed this can be true of most personal friendships of Christians and the non-committed, even when not involved in the activities above. And now we can see why.

Friends naturally try to share all their significant interests. When there is a difference of religion, with one friend being a committed believer and the other being uninterested or ignorant or unbelieving, the latter is likely to feel uncomfortable and even embarrassed about their lack of what means so much to the former. Therefore, friendship of itself, apart from the activities suggested above, will generate some cognitive dissonance, especially when the Christian's witness has *Nurtured* his or her friend's *Sense of God*. Indeed it might be thought that our elaborate typology, and the range of church activities we have proposed above to match it, are superfluous: why should not religious communication rely on friendship alone?

However this is not so. One obvious fact is that many of our Communicatees will have *no* Christian friends to *Nurture their Sense of God* and to motivate them. Sadly some Christians are so inward-looking and mutually preoccupied that they have no time or energy for a ministry of friendship to the non-committed. Again not every friendship will of itself generate the motivation required. Some friendships focus only on superficial or highly specific interests: religion and politics are excluded from the relationship and are never mentioned or discussed. It is, though, hard to see how any deep friendship can long survive without differences, over any matter so pervasive and existential as religious faith, at least being aired and brought into the open. But of course the friends may then agree to differ and never to mention the subject again: in which case no dissonance will emerge or endure, if it has begun to appear.

Hence friendship alone cannot be relied on to have the desired effect. So taking part in joint activities with several Christians will be needed to generate cognitive dissonance over the spiritual differences they have with the Communicatees, in contrast to the common ground believers and Communicatees share. Nonetheless in many cases these deep divergences will overflow into the friendships that will grow up around the common activities: and thus the motivation, working together stimulates, will be reinforced by the cognitive dissonance which arises between people, who are now also personal friends.

(iii) Applying Myers-Briggs in Communication

How may a strategy for the Stage of *Motivation* be devised by a Christian (or other faith) Communicator? In the first place, Communicators need to be familiar with Myers-Briggs and to have been assessed themselves by the Instrument. They must then realise how they are perhaps partly like the Communicatee in type terms and partly different. In the general population about 75% are E and another 75% are S,[17] whereas Christian congregations and clergy are much more to be found at the other end of the polarities concerned.[18] In a few cases, as at the beginning of a course, it may be possible to assess properly the type of the Communicatee by asking them to complete a test Instrument or the Myers-Briggs Type Indicator. Most frequently Communicators will have to be content with their own experienced and intuitive impression as to the type and temperament of the Communicatees.

Secondly it may sometimes be possible to select the appropriate motivational approach in the light of the type and temperament of a group or an individual the Communicator wishes to get to learn and to explore. But it is far more likely that as a pastor, teacher, evangelist, nurturer, lecturer or tutor (dialogists are excluded, because motivation in Inter-Faith

Dialogue may be taken for granted), the Communicator will encounter a mixed stream of people of every type and temperament. The best policy will then be to offer a variety of approach and stimulus which will appeal sooner or later to every type and temperament represented in those contacted. Thus the programme of a local church or religious organisation needs diversity, taking full advantage of the feasts and fasts of the Christian year and the multi-faceted life that should characterise a vigorous and enterprising Christian community.

In every endeavour undertaken, attention must be paid to its motivational potential for some or all of the types and temperaments of those involved. For work with children, practising Christians and even committed Christians, *Nurture* must take advantage of every opportunity church life affords to motivate religious *Learning* and *Exploration* in different ways to suit peoples' varying needs. Teachers may learn something from this approach to motivate older pupils in *Religious Education* (though with the young, type and temperament are not yet fixed but relatively fluid.)[19] The evangelist, who hopes to present the Gospel to those outside the church, will have to be opportunistic in seizing every chance to provoke interest, in the multiplicity of ways outlined above, given the variety of type and temperament there is bound to be in any constituency he or she is working with. (The application of this point to higher education will be discussed in Chapter VIII.)

In the third place, it is important for the Communicator to be clear about an important distinction that has so far been implicit in our discussion, and now needs to be made explicit. Sometimes people will be motivated through an activity distinct from the *Learning* and *Exploration* that will follow it. They get involved in what attracts them with committed Christians or with the Communicator and the latter can then exploit the motivational potential in the situation to encourage attendance or interest in courses e.g. in Alpha courses in church or in reading books or watching TV or videos about the Christian faith.

Quite often, however, the *Motivating* is not a distinct enterprise from the *Teaching, Learning* or *Exploration*. The Communicator decides to lay on a course or to offer home visits as in the Good News Down The Street[20] and the motivational activity is an aspect of the project, such as the presentation or publicity or mode of learning involved. Presenting a religious message via music or drama or video or books *both* effects the *Learning* and incites the *Exploration and* at the same time *Motivates* people of an appropriate type or temperament to attend functions and to be stimulated to make the effort the exercise requires if it is to be profitable.

This analysis leads to the final point about our Stage of *Motivation*. We have discussed above many kinds of stimulus which may provide the spark to ignite the fire of interest and to present the discrepancy, puzzle, paradox or question that effects the cognitive dissonance, moving people to act. Though these stimuli can precede in time the subsequent Stages of *Learning* and of *Exploration*, they may be coincident with these Stages but obviously cannot come later than the times they are needed. Further, *Motivation*, whatever prompts it, must continue long enough for the Communicatee to have reason to attend and to make time to attend gatherings (and thus also satisfy the *Opportunity* Background Condition which merely makes attendance possible); to pay attention to a speaker, book or film etc. and to work, so as to gain knowledge; and to utilise it in active *Exploration*. Since people will not do these things unless they are motivated, *Motivation* is logically prior, even when simultaneous with the action it offers reason to undertake. This is why the Stage of *Motivation* comes before the Stages of *Learning* and *Exploration*. Differential stimuli are given to the Communicatee, once his or her *Sense of God* has been *nurtured* in the previous Stage. Then he or she proceeds to the *Learning* and *Exploration* Stages they undergo, because *Motivation* has been aroused.

(iv) Other Categorisations

So far we have discussed motivating different types of people by taking advantage of the Myers-Briggs typology. Other ways of classifying human beings could be developed, which might also assist with religious communication. Gender and Social Class suggested themselves and have already been considered in other contexts.[21] The approach already used in Chapter IV has been to tackle these social and personal differences as a way of removing obstacles to the autonomy the Communicatee needs.[22]

An alternative, as hinted earlier,[23] is to take the Communicatee more as we find him or her, despite the lack of autonomy involved, and to discover what will appeal to people with qualities of each kind within a classification. By this means, the Communicator can develop ranges of activity and experience that provide for the mature adult the non-religious contact with the religious community, that generates cognitive dissonance.

With respect to gender, relative attraction of femininity to religion is well-known and nothing needs adding here.[24] As we suggested above, with typical men, approaches based on masculinity can be employed.[25] What we need to point out in this context of *Motivation* is just how they work and could be effective. The heroic qualities of Jesus and the Saints (or of comparable figures in other faiths) may be stressed. Ancillary activities of a recreational or sporting or cultural nature linked to churches may be developed which involve men and give a setting where dissonance may come about, once a *Sense of God* has been *nurtured*. Practical, hands-on work, DIY on buildings, gardening in grounds, fund-raising, vehicle maintenance, community development, youth work and many other enterprises may afford a context where religious people meet male Communicatees and witness to them; and interest may thus be fired by realisation of the gap between faith and its absence in those who are working side by side.

Where social class is concerned this approach unfortunately cannot be developed because so little is known about the real factors that underlie socio-economic differentials in religious behaviour. There is indeed some recent suggestion that such differences are shrinking to vanishing point[26] and it may be possible to ignore them in future. Where however class differences may appear to be pertinent, as in Verbal Ability, and assuming that some people are lacking in this respect and unalterable in the foreseeable future, we would encourage non-verbal approaches to communication, so far as this is possible for a religion that has a message at its heart and a belief-system to commend.

Perhaps basic ideas at the heart of a faith may be intuitively grasped or inductively learnt by contact with visual symbols, mime, art, or music, drama or the media, or liturgy. Such encounters with the religious Communicator or the faithful could engender dissonance and so *Motivation* at an implicit level. Further speculation in this area is profitless but research and experiment in non-verbal communication – in so far as this is possible – are urgent. In the meantime the basic methodology for *Motivation* we recommend is clear. Once the *Sense of God* is *Nurtured* in someone, find points of contact with the faith that will appeal to the kind of person a Communicatee is; develop these, and cognitive dissonance should emerge and make him or her ready and willing to move on to our Stages of *Learning* and *Exploration*.

Notes

[1] Myers, I. B. with Myers, P. B. (1980), *Gifts Differing,* Consulting Psychological Press Books, Palo Alto, California; Keirsey, P. and Bates, M. (1978), *Please Understand Me* Prometheus Nemesis Book Co., Del Mar.

[2] v. 2 (iii), **4** (iii).

[3] v. **4** (iii).

[4] (1921), *Psychological Types,* Princeton University Press, Princeton, New Jersey.
[5] Myers, op. cit., **Pt. I**; Keirsey and Bates, op. cit.; Grant, Thompson, Clarke, op. cit.; Keating, C. J. (1987), *Who We Are Is How We Pray,* 23A Publications Mystic, Connecticut.
[6] Myers, op. cit., **4;** Keirsey and Bates, op. cit., 14–16; Grant, Thompson, Clarke, op. cit., 16; Keating, op. cit., 7,32–51.
[7] Myers, op. cit., **7**; Keirsey and Bates, op. cit., 22–28; Grant, Thompson, Clarke, op. cit., 17; Keating, op. cit., 12, 93–115.
[8] Myers, op. cit., **8**; Keirsey and Bates, op. cit., 16–19; Grant, Thompson, Clarke, op. cit., 17, **2**; Keating, op. cit., 9,52–72.
[9] Myers, op. cit., **6**; Keirsey and Bates, op. cit., 20–22; Grant, Thompson, Clarke, op. cit., *18*–19; Keating, op. cit.,10ff.,73–92.
[10] Myers, op. cit., 4–6; Keirsey and Bates, op. cit., **2**.
[11] v. **4** (iii).
[12] Gumbel, N. (1994), *Telling Others: the Alpha Initiative, Kingsway* Publications Ltd., Eastbourne, (cf. also Brierley (2000), op. cit., 174 for Alpha take-up); also cf. Cottrell, S., Croft, S., Finney, J., Lawson, F. and Warren, R. (1996*), Emmaus: The Way of Faith,* British and Foreign Bible Society, National Society, Church House Publishing, London/Swindon.
[13] Newbigin, (1984), op. cit., **5**; Montefiore, H. (1992), *The Gospel and Contemporary Culture,* Mowbray, London.
[14] Reeves, M. Ed. (1999*), Christian Thinking and Social Order,* Cassell, London, **Pt. II 3**; (1942), Christian Newsletter No 154 Supplement, 7 October.
[15] v. **4** (iii).
[16] Clarke, J. (1995), *Evangelism that really works,* S. P. C. K., London, 148–149; Finney, op. cit., 36–37, 43–47.
[17] Keirsey and Bates, op. cit., 25.
[18] Duncan, B., (1991), *Church of England Clergy and Laity,* Manchester Cathedral, (compared to US base populations) (unpublished tables).
[19] Grant, Thompson, Clarke, op. cit., 20–22.
[20] Wooderson, M. (1982), *No.9 Grove Books,* Bramcote, Notts.
[21] v. **2** (iii) and (iv).
[22] v. **4** (iii).
[23] v. **2** (iv).
[24] v. **2** (iv).
[25] v. **2** (iv).
[26] Bruce, op cit., 44.

Chapter 7

Learning, Exploration and Commitment

In this Chapter we shall consider Stages VI, VII and VIII in our Theory. We shall discuss *Learning, Exploration* and *Commitment* in religion. We shall clarify what the Communicatee needs to learn, if he or she is to be able effectively to proceed to *Exploration*. Then we analyse the character of *Exploration* and argue that, if it is not to be a purely subjective assessment, we need to be able to offer some agreed and defensible set of criteria for religious truth. Finally, we shall show the kinds of commitment required by the different species of religious communication that we have distinguished.[1]

(i) Learning

Can we now specify *what* must be learnt about Christianity (or any other theistic faith) for the purposes of *Evangelism*, the *Nurture* of children and of adults, *Religious Education,* the *Academic Study of Religion* and *Ministerial Formation,* and what content *Inter-Faith Dialogue* takes for granted? Obviously what will serve each of these distinct enterprises we have distinguished will differ very considerably. Clearly account will also have to be taken of the differing ages, abilities, backgrounds and temperaments[2] of the Communicatees. There will also be, in practice, constraints of time, resources and teaching approaches when we decide what *Learning* it is feasible to bring about. Sometimes it may be possible to proceed quickly to *Exploration* on the basis of a slight amount of *Learning.* Otherwise further knowledge acquisition will go hand in hand with answering questions raised by the Communicatees in their quest,[3] always remembering that logically you cannot explore in ignorance.

Nonetheless it seems fruitful to sketch out a basic, ruling-conception of what has to be learnt as a norm or ideal, what knowledge a programme of teaching should aim to inculcate. From this ruling conception we may derive criteria for deciding what the Communicatee needs to know. The knowledge required will of course have to be modified by the limits and the constraints just set out.

Our suggestion is that the Communicatee needs to learn what it is to be a Christian (or to be an adherent of another faith) in terms of the ruling-conception of that religion to be presented in Stage VI. This conception has four dimensions.

First, a religion like Christianity is a belief-system. Its basic beliefs need to be known, understood and the case for them appreciated. For this purpose we propose, as part of our ruling conception, acquaintance with the basic Christian beliefs as expressed in the Creeds, which have commanded nearly universal assent by the whole church across the world and down the centuries.[4] This credal content needs supplementing in three ways to complete the cognitive dimension of being a Christian.

The Communicatee should firstly be familiar with the biblical background the Creeds presuppose. Second, the essential concepts employed in the belief system must be grasped so that it can be understood. Here we need to distinguish the essential concepts of a faith from those which are inessential and technical.[5] For example sin is an essential concept but distinctions between mortal and venial or formal and material sin are not: these belong to academic or pastoral theology. (Another concept, the underlying, categorial notion of God has already been treated.)[6] These essential concepts, which are crucial to religious belief when used analogically or metaphorically, come from everyday life: examples are father, son, life, death, body and blood. The possession of many such concepts required by the Communicatee will be ensured by the *Background Condition* of *Verbal Ability*.[7]

Thirdly, since the Creeds contain no mention of the Eucharist and its meaning and institution, which are central to most Christian belief about worship, some knowledge of these matters must be added to the cognitive dimension of what is involved in being a Christian.

The second dimension in this ruling conception of being a Christian is moral. The Communicatee must learn what values, norms and rules for living belong to Christian (or other faith) commitment and what behaviour is expected of a believer. The Communicator needs to set out what it means to love God and your neighbour in the modern world, in terms of politics and personal relationships.

The third dimension the Communicatee needs to know about is worship and prayer and how to take part in these activities. Learners must be able to share in corporate and private devotion, if they so desire, with whatever background beliefs and concepts may be pertinent.

Fourth comes the affective, emotional or attitudinal dimension of this ruling conception of being a Christian.[8] Communicatees must be acquainted with how believers feel in response to God and Jesus as believers' perceptions of these figures are governed by Christian belief. Emotions are generated and constituted by reactions to certain situations seen in particular ways.[9] If, for instance, the Gospel is apprehended as good news, the normal human response is that positive, intense, affect or feeling we call joy. In order to gain familiarity with this aspect of what being a Christian means, the Communicatee's imagination has to be stimulated to produce a sympathetic entry into the Christian's worldview and empathy with the believer's situation. Should the

Communicatee later actually come to *Commitment*, he or she will share in this emotional aspect of the life of faith.

To introduce our Communicatee to these four so very different dimensions of what being a Christian involves is the critical requirement of our Stage of *Learning*. What is next important for our purposes is to see how this ruling conception of being a Christian is related to our seven Species of Religious Communication.

Evangelism and *Religious Education* require Communicatees to have this ruling conception before they are in a position to explore it and perhaps to decide for or against commitment. This option of the many-faceted Christian way of life must be familiar prior to one being able to evaluate it. As was said above, it is not necessary to know all and *then* explore, but each issue to be investigated can only be appraised rationally and responsibly given an adequate body of background knowledge. Perhaps the school child or potential convert will have to travel far along the road our Theory charts before they can seriously assess Christianity (or another religion) as a possible faith to live by.

Inter-Faith Dialogue, the *Nurture* of adults, the *Academic Study of Religion* and *Ministerial Formation presuppose* our ruling conception as their starting-point. In the case of *Nurture* it is assumed the Christian Communicatee possesses the ruling conception (or some of it), has explored this and is committed to it. *Nurture* consists in further *Learning* and *Exploration* of elements in a person's conception of what it is to be a Christian which are not so well known or in pursuing aspects of its several dimensions in never-ending depth and detail. Such learning can fill the remainder of the Communicatee's life on earth and maybe into the hereafter. With *Inter-Faith Dialogue,* this ruling conception of one faith is what equips a believer to make a sympathetic and intelligent approach to another believer possessed of the corresponding ruling conception of his or her own faith. Dialogue cannot usefully proceed from ignorance on either side or both.

Now the *Academic Study of Religion* requires the same grasp of the ruling conception, but without belief in it or commitment to it, and then builds on its cognitive elements, advancing learning in accordance with the procedures of scholarship and branching out into the special disciplines of Theology and Religious Studies. *Ministerial Formation*, as we shall suggest, must assume commitment, despite proceeding within the *Academic Study of Religion,* but with that commitment suspended for the sake of argument when study is pursued in its first phase within Higher Education. This commitment is, however, renewed when *Ministerial Formation* becomes in its second phase a kind of *Nurture* (of adults). In both phases the ruling conception remains the base from which to advance.

Finally *Child Nurture* so presents the ruling-conception as to take account of children as practising but not yet committed Christians. Young children hear what the Christian faith and life is and how to live it. They practise the faith in which they are being nurtured. Yet the belief element is presented at first clearly and firmly as what 'we' believe and then more self-consciously as what Christian adults, parents and teachers believe. As young people become mature, they should be encouraged to be autonomous, to stand back to decide whether they too can properly believe and, if so, to make a personal commitment.[10] The churches' children begin by being inducted into the beliefs, worship, prayer, values and conduct expected of Christians, then make up their minds on the basic credal truth-claims and choose whether to continue in the faith of their fathers and mothers. Thus they enter gradually and in stages into what needs to be learnt, our ruling conception of what being a Christian is.

(ii) Exploration

What exactly is involved in a person, who is relatively well-informed about what it is to be a Christian (or a follower of another religion), coming to explore faith as an option for himself or herself to which they may feel ready to commit themselves? As with what we said about *Learning*, the quantity, quality, level, timing and sophistication of a person's voyage of spiritual discovery will vary enormously according to the age, education, background, opportunity and circumstances of the Communicatee. However, we shall here sketch in an ideal of what *Exploration* of Christianity (or of some other theistic faith) should be like.

A fundamental distinction has to be made at the outset between two interpretations of a religion. The objective interpretation regards it as a way of life, full of myths, symbols and rituals, but also crucially containing 'public truths', independent facts about the universe, an account of reality. The other subjective interpretation also sees a faith as a way of life, but whose symbols, myths and rituals have no necessary descriptive reference to transcendent reality beyond the everyday world of science and common sense.[11] These two interpretations are, of course, the extreme opposite ends of a scale or spectrum or what sociologists call ideal types. There are many intermediate positions between them and most adherents of a faith will have a mixture of both types in varying proportions. Elaborate belief-systems will not be on the surface of many peoples' faith but must be presupposed if the way of life they adopt is to make sense of experience. Symbols, myths and rituals may largely have a life of their own, but can seldom logically govern conduct and feeling if there is no purchase on reality, on how this world, and the world to come, actually are. We shall consider separately how each interpretation requires a different mode of exploration, even though in practice these two modes will nearly always be combined in differing degrees.

On the second subjective, existential interpretation of a faith, exploration is simple. A person considers, by means of discussion, reflection, dialogue, role-plays and other projective methods whether a given religious way of life appeals and attracts. They might further investigate by trying out living by this faith for a while, provisionally committing themselves to it. Does this religion suit me and help me to cope with life? Does this faith illuminate the human condition and enable us to live well in the face of life and death, good and evil, joy and suffering? Suppose the explorer does return a positive answer to these questions. A little further reflection may suggest that unless this faith has a backing in how the world is and accurately characterises the human condition, correctly solving the great riddles of life, the help and illumination sought may well turn out to be illusory. So the questioner has reason to move to the more objective interpretation of the content of faith.

On the first objective interpretation, that a religion makes serious truth-claims, *Exploration* will comprise assessing these same claims for truth. If such a faith appears to be true in its main essentials, that is a reason to adopt it and to respond to it positively, even though it does not seem to be the most attractive and enticing way of life. Classic religion is not held to be about success or pleasure. What shall it profit a man if he gain the whole world and lose his own soul?[12] Conceivably considerations concerning the next world may also be relevant, especially if the arguments are inconclusive: compare Pascal's wager.[13] Pascal argued that, if we really cannot decide by reason whether God exists, it was rational to take a bet on the infinite gain for the individual, on the supposition that Christian belief is objectively true and the individual puts their faith in it!

Now it should be noted that most Christians and followers of other faiths down the ages have supposed that religion is about objective truth. Those today who disagree do so usually only *after* they have rejected religious truth-claims as false, unwarranted or meaningless.[14] In view of these considerations, it seems unfair to the Communicatees not to give them the chance to explore divers religions as possibly true accounts of the cosmos. Academic and educational values require this approach in *Religious Education, Academic Study* and *Ministerial Formation*. For Communicators, working with Christian values of integrity and autonomy, or with similar values from other faiths, a parallel concern for truth will apply to *Inter-Faith Dialogue, Nurture* of adults and children, and *Evangelism*. Also it is likely that pupils, students, young or older Christians being nurtured, or beginning to be interested in God and matters to do with theism, will ask questions about religious truth. If no account is given of such an objective interpretation of a faith and what it means to explore it, the questioners will be sold short and not be given a chance to pursue issues of truth which they consider important.

We have already claimed that the Communicatee should learn what are the main Christian beliefs, understand them and appreciate the case for them. How then does he or she explore their truth? In science the educated person knows he or she can appeal to results of crucial experiments and observations; people also have some awareness of moral argument and reasons that are appropriate to give in support of ethical conclusions. What are the corresponding considerations in theistic religion? The Communicator needs to be able to offer the Communicatees truth-criteria, criteria for determining religious truth, for the Communicatees to apply for themselves. Applying such criteria in the controversial area distinctive of religious claims is what *Exploration* now means. All we can do in this discussion is to propose such a set of criteria and to hope debate will one day lead toward a consensus of Communicators, theologians and philosophers, if *Exploration* is to be a serious proposition. So very tentatively we formulate below a group of criteria that seem to us adequate for our purposes.[15]

One proposal for criteria to assess religion has recently been made by Hobson and Edwards.[16] They borrow the tests of agreement with data, consistency, scope and fertility that Barbour,[17] in a powerful discussion of science and religion, has suggested are widely recognised by scientists to be significant in evaluating models and theories. So the theological explorer would ask of a faith whether it agrees with experience; is coherent and self-consistent both internally and externally with other knowledge; whether this faith covers more or less all our human concerns; and how it casts light on wider issues and new questions and opens up fresh fields of enquiry.

However, it seems to us that these criteria are not satisfactory in assessing religious claims, whether particular doctrines or whole faiths. Indeed these truth-tests Hobson and Edwards advocate are both too narrow and too wide and do not adequately apply to theism or to the specific beliefs within a faith. Every follower of a world religion will doubtless think their own faith passes the Barbour tests with flying colours: it all depends on where you come from and on your existing outlook, doubtless as shaped by your spiritual background. Hobson and Edwards concede only a 'sophisticated relativism' will result rather than truth:[18] that is, wide cross-cultural agreement on what holds in the spiritual sphere but expressed in the differing languages of many faiths.

Clearly one major issue for *Exploration* is the theism several of the great world faiths share. It is hard to see how the Barbour criteria apply to the existence of God. Perhaps internal consistency does, and we shall build this element into our own proposals below.[19] But to compare theism, as it underlies several living religions, with atheism or humanism in terms of comprehensiveness, fertility and agreement with data, is not a profitable exercise. How can one possibly judge in such matters, except in ways that reflect one's own starting point and prejudices?

This application of Barbour's criteria by Hobson and Edwards is not only too narrow for theism as such but too wide for use with the tenets of a particular faith. How can the agreement with data test be applied to credal items like the resurrection and incarnation in Christianity or the law-giving or creation in all the Abrahamic religions? Ghosts of the old falsification controversies of a generation ago will arise and the result will be indeterminate.[20] Whatever hostile data are brought forward, believers will always be able to explain them and to save appearances. It will be difficult to apply the criteria of comprehensiveness and fecundity to propositions of narrow scope and unclear how to appraise the multiple implications of these propositions. Consistency, whether within a doctrine or with other knowledge we accept, as we have said above, and will employ in our own proposals. But the other criteria fit much more comfortably with whole religions or theories or dogmas than to specific claims such as the claim that Jesus rose from the dead, Moses gave the law or Muhammad faithfully reproduced the messages Gabriel gave him.

Again many claims within a faith are moral or historical and truth-tests for these seem obviously to come from ethics or historiography. Scientific standards like Barbour's are inappropriate both to these claims *and* to those about God. Above all the appeal to revelation is ignored. Religious doctrines in the great theistic faiths are alleged to derive from God's self-disclosures in ancient history and scripture. Debates in the history of theology have largely turned in the past on what can be truly supported by the sources of religious belief that are held to be God's making himself known to the prophets and to holy men and women. It is hard to see how *Exploration* can proceed in our communicative enterprises today without appeal to the foundation of religious truth as this foundation has always been conceived. What God has declared, where and whether his declaration is to be found, are the crucial issues in determining the doctrines of a faith. Science is a fundamentally different enterprise, surveying and appraising current experimental and other observable data by criteria such as Barbour's. Religion is about God and what can be learnt of him from nature, history and experience; and from his own revelation of himself, if there be any such.

To establish religious truth-criteria it seems to us that, therefore, we must turn to revelation; we must examine its identification and presuppositions in theism; and while we do all this, not neglect Barbour's valuable emphasis on consistency and coherence. We must also take seriously moral and historical elements in religious claims. As well as particular doctrines within a faith and thus that faith as a whole, our criteria, to be satisfactory, must also enable the Communicatee to adjudicate in some rational fashion between the great religions of the world and their specific tenets.

(iii) Religious Truth-Criteria

The truth-criteria we propose fall into three groups: pre-religious, intra-religious and inter-religious. The 'pre-religious' apply non-religious tests to religious claims. Any putative religious proposition needs to pass these tests for possible truth, before distinctively religious yardsticks are applied. Then, assuming a theistic religion is presented as a distinguishable belief-system, as an integral whole, 'intra-religious' truth-criteria, peculiar to one faith, are brought to bear on the religious statements of that faith, these statements defined as those that directly or indirectly relate to God. Lastly because today any serious exploration of one faith, like Christianity, is difficult without at least looking at other great faiths represented in Britain, and which offer profitable contrasts and comparisons with Christianity, we need to have 'inter-religious' truth-criteria, to determine the truth of religious claims per se and not just as an element in one particular religious belief-system. It should also be noted, though, that claims such as 'God exists' do not arise in the context of one faith only or indeed of any faith and that the truth of such claims may be supported by considerations arising from within several faiths or outside of any. (It is also assumed, in a post-modern age, that at least the possibility of the objective, universal truth of beliefs from one or more grand narratives should be considered and that we do not have to surrender to fashionable relativism.)[21]

(a) Pre-Religious Criteria

The first pre-religious criterion is 'logical'. A religious claim must be consistent, coherent and intelligible to stand at all as a serious descriptive statement, or even as being implicit in some attitude or emotion. Such a claim must also be compatible with other forms of human knowledge, for instance, with the physical sciences over theological accounts of creation: there is not only the traditional conundrum of the compatibility of evolution by natural selection with Genesis (or other Scriptures) but also the origin of life and the soul/body problem – is the theological doctrine of humanity consistent with behaviourism, physicalism and brain/mind identity theories? Is free-will required by faith and is this consonant with determinism and computer models of the brain? Is the origin of the universe in the big bang capable of being harmonised with creation by God? How does eschatology relate to the future of the universe as disclosed by astronomy and cosmology? Can prayer in principle modify the course of events in a world governed by physical law? Can God change the outcome of history or heal the sick who are terminally ill? Is there any room for providence in the flow of phenomena?

An obvious example of internal inconsistency to which our criterion will seem to apply is the Trinity: how can God be both three and one together? Can there be a plurality of omnipotent persons, such that they cannot destroy or mutually frustrate each other? (We shall largely give in our exposition Christian examples; cases from other faiths could be supplied by their theologians). Again if Jesus is God and man, how can he be one person? If he is human, could he have come down from the cross? If he is God, how could he have been unable to do so? Did he simultaneously have the limited knowledge of a first-century Jew and the omniscience of the divine Word? Such puzzles and paradoxes, ancient and modern, show there is plenty of work for the Communicatee employing our first 'logical' criterion in exploring religious truth.

The second pre-religious criterion is 'moral'. If a religious belief contains or implies moral values, it is open to criticism on moral grounds. (We assume here the minimal claim that some form of independent, secular reasoning in ethics has some plausibility and that the Communicatee has some moral convictions.) Examples to which this test is relevant are Original Guilt, the Penal Substitutionary Theory of the Atonement and Eternal Hell for the damned. And above all there is the problem of evil and of innocent suffering? The 'moral' criterion is applied in *Exploration* precisely in seeing whether claims that God is good, righteous and loving in the ordinary sense of these terms can possibly be true.

The third pre-religious criterion is 'historical'. Where religious claims involve history, that history must be substantiated by the tests of historical scholarship. For example, can enough be known of Jesus to identify him by some minimum description – e.g. suffered under Pontius Pilate – as the specific man in whom the Word was made flesh? Without such a foundation the Incarnation has no real bite or cutting edge. Again did Moses really lead Israel out of Egypt and was Jerusalem rescued from Sennacherib and did it fall to Nebuchadnezzar?

Then there is a special problem with miracles. A priori considerations need advancing to show that miracles could have occurred in theologically significant stretches of history.[22] Thus it becomes possible to apply historical criteria and to compare alleged miraculous events with normal happenings in the same context, and so discrimination among signs and wonders can be attempted. For instance, if the Nativity stories are unlikely to be historical fact, the Virgin Birth as one of them becomes questionable, even if a priori support for it as a miracle can be argued. And the same goes for bodily resurrection and the empty tomb, and for the physical healings of Christ and his nature miracles. These must all be placed in the surrounding contexts of other non-miraculous events and assessed accordingly.

(b) Intra-Religious Criteria

There are two tests. Either or both together assess particular claims within a faith. The first is the 'validity of philosophical argument' for the belief in question. An example is natural theology with its reasons for the existence and nature of God, provided these are considered cogent.[23] The second, alternative, criterion is 'foundational'. Religions appeal to their founders for knowledge of God; to the life and teaching of these figures; to the reflection of the first followers on the founder's teaching; and to later development of the tradition thus arising. Often this deposit of faith is formulated in special documents or 'Scriptures'. The Bible is an example. The foundational criterion asks whether a particular claim can be substantiated from Scripture or tradition, with statements in these acting as premises.

It is claimed that the foundation-teaching of a religion contains a true revelation of God. In our discussion we now assume natural theology does yield cogent arguments for God's existence and nature. Then it is possible to produce reasons for the truth of the foundation-teachings. We present very briefly three possible examples of such reasons.

First, if a good God creates the world with a purpose for rational creatures, it is likely he will make this known to them.[24] If evolution is so providentially guided as to give rise to intelligent beings, whose minds have powers of reason that must have been implicit in the original matter, it may be the creator's aim to have creatures that can know and respond to him and his purposes. And it would be paradoxical and absurd if God had allowed the world's great religions to have arisen and to have taught so much about him, if this teaching is totally wide of the mark! Of course some allowance must be made for human freedom to err, which is doubtless part of the explanation of why much in all the world's faiths is erroneous. But God's purpose cannot be entirely defeated, surely, by humanity's fallibility, if he is all good and all wise. Should then the whole of the alleged disclosures of God in the world's great faiths, in their impressive unity and variety, be totally misdirected, the creator's apparent objective in eliciting the human race's co-operation would be frustrated and nullified. Such a reductio ad absurdum suggests the possibility that providence may have so steered mankind's religious development that some of the ideas of men and women about God could be on the right lines. Hence there is a prima facie case for their truth.

Second, the testimony of a witness is the more plausible if part of his story can be independently corroborated. To be able to check up on what the traveller from foreign parts says on his return, by reference to another type of witness or to indirect evidence from a different direction, will increase the weight we shall attach to his report. Part of the foundation-teachings consists in a doctrine of creation. If this latter claim is also supported by natural theology which, in arguing for God's existence, implicitly argues for the createdness of the universe, corroboration is found to support the remainder of the scriptures' testimony to God's character and actions. The Bible and the Scriptures of other faiths tell us God made the world. This truth is expressed in a variety of images and mythology. If, however, the core claim involved of origination ex nihilo and preservation by an invisible and intangible agent can be sustained by philosophical reasoning to the effect that a creator must be postulated, it is reasonable to give weight to the vast diversity of other doctrines about God contained in these religious foundation- teachings.

Third, one plank in the case for God's existence is the appeal to religious experiences. We have already seen the force of this argument.[25] Prophets, mystics, seers and gurus have a vivid sense of the presence and closeness of God. He is always disclosing to them, they claim, further truth about his nature and purpose to pass on to their followers. So it is not surprising that experiences pointing to God's existence sometimes come in close association with other teaching about God such as the world's great religions afford. If such experiences do really testify to God's objective existence, why should the accompanying teaching not also give insight into God's nature and purposes?[26] Hence we get a third argument in support of our foundational criterion that locating a theological claim within the Scriptures, or being able to derive it from such a source, is to have prima facie reason for accepting its truth.

Such arguments, if they were to be fully developed in a work concerned with the truth of revelation in the great faiths, would support a religion's appeal to its foundation-teaching and so would support our foundational criterion. But there is a most important corollary to this claim we must underline. These arguments, if valid, will support *equally* the truth of the several putative revelations in the major theistic religions: if any are valid, all are! Hence inter-religious truth criteria are urgently required for the explorer to use in discussing the array of teachings that can be derived from the foundation-teachings and Scriptures of the principal religions of the world, which claim to speak truthfully about God, the Creator and object of the world's religious experience (or of a greater part of it, including also the testimony of those who have experienced the Ultimate in non-personal ways, as in some western and eastern mysticism).

(c) Inter-Religious Truth-Criteria

Arising from our discussion, three criteria emerge as possible. First is 'unopposed attestation'. Where the same doctrine can be supported from the Scriptures of more than one faith, and where the same belief is not opposed elsewhere in the several faiths' foundation-teachings, it can be regarded as well-established. Examples are God's goodness, wisdom, judgement and providence in Christianity, Judaism, Islam, Sikhism and possibly in some strands of Hinduism, as well as revelation about prayer and the afterlife. Disclosures of divine law also agree sufficiently in ethical essentials to present commonalities to be assessed by our moral criterion. (And historical claims which overlap e.g. ancient Israel in the Christian Old Testament, Jewish Bible and the Qur'an – can be evaluated severally by historical criteria.)

Where the teachings of world religions appear to conflict, a second criterion of inter-religious debate emerges, that of 'accommodation'. This states that, since all the foundation-teachings of the great religions may contain truth about God, as much as possible of the traditions should be harmonised and preserved. That formulation is to be preferred which best accommodates divergent tenets within a coherent whole.

A contemporary theology, on the philosophical foundations argued for here, would see truth from God inclusively, coming via many channels in the world's Scriptures. For example Christian claims about the Trinity and Incarnation might be accommodated to Muslim criticisms of Jesus being Son of God, by claiming that these criticisms represent legitimate and true objections to various misconstruals of the classic formulae of the Church Fathers and Councils. Thus the Qur'an objects Jesus cannot be God because he has bodily weaknesses;[27] and cannot be the Son of God because God cannot physically beget a son;[28] nor produce a second independent divine being alongside himself.[29] These denials a Christian believer can gladly accept because they do not touch the orthodox formulation of the Incarnation, on which the Qur'an is silent. Christ's bodily weaknesses belong to his human nature alone and do not interfere with his divine nature, of which God the Son has emptied himself, in so far as Jesus leads a human life; the Son's begetting is an eternal and non-physical process of generation; and he shares a unity of one substance with the other persons of the Trinity, so only *one* God results. In such ways truth purportedly revealed by God in the Qur'an can be accommodated alongside Christian claims about Jesus and our second criterion is thus applied and might be thought to be satisfied.

Another example is that the Transcendent Reality beyond the cosmos is sometimes seen as a personal Creator, sometimes as a non-personal Absolute. One accommodation favoured in the Christian tradition is to assert that God is ultimately personal but can be apprehended in some mystical experience as non-personal. An alternative Hindu accommodation is the reverse: the personal deity experienced is an anthropomorphic projection and the true Ultimate lies beyond all being and is an infinite non-personal Absolute.[30]

It is hard to see how to resolve this duality of interpretations, each appearing to accommodate divergent revelations, unless an appeal is made to philosophical argument. What kind of conclusion does natural theology support? Metaphysical reasoning may lead to making a transcendent personal agent appear more plausible than an ultimate non-personal force or field. If God is postulated as creator to explain the ordered universe we find and from which we believe we can obtain objective knowledge, it is hard to see how a creative process can be other than the act of a personal agent. Can a force or field or an abstraction do anything real? Thus we finally reach the third inter-religious criterion, using again one of the intra-religious criteria, that of the 'validity of philosophical argument'.

It may appear strange and paradoxical to use a scheme of argument supportive of the revelation of a personal God to furnish inter-religious truth-criteria for the enquirer to apply to both theistic and non-theistic religions. Two responses can be made to this difficulty. One is that if faiths that claim to give teaching about a personal God contain some truth about reality, it may well be a fact that such a God makes himself known also, in disguised and indirect forms, in religions that do not focus on a personal deity. Secondly, the application of our religious truth-criterion of philosophical argument to the metaphysical claims a non-theistic faith makes about the Transcendent, such as Brahman in Hinduism or Sunyata in Mahayana Buddhism, may perfectly well yield independent religious truths about the cosmos: and these may have to be held in conjunction with the claims of theistic faith and integrated with them in the best accommodation possible. Thus it may be possible to know by experience the universe as Sunyata, as a flow of preconceptualised phenomena, utterly free of our egotistic projections; or one may be enabled to perceive Brahman as 'being-consciousness-bliss', and still to conceive these realities as the face of creation or as contours of a personal divine agent, God.[31]

We must now round off our discussion of truth-criteria by considering what happens if natural theology and the arguments we have given in support of a religion's foundation-teachings are deemed invalid, implausible or inappropriate. The pre-religious criteria remain unchanged. It may then be assumed on faith, if the explorer wishes, that God exists and that he has made himself known in a specific foundation-teaching. The intra-religious foundational criterion can then still be used in testing the beliefs of a particular religion against its Scriptures or foundation-teaching. The decision to make this act of faith in God and in a revelation could follow from employing our earlier subjective, existential and pragmatic mode of exploration to find an attractive way of life. Presumably, also, choice of faith, or of which religion to adhere to, can be brought under this mixed form of *Exploration,* bringing together both our earlier interpretations of these notions. Thus quite a substantial content is left for the Stage of *Exploration*, which can then survive the alleged collapse of philosophical arguments for theism and for objectively true foundation-teachings, on a basis of 'Fideism', as the approach of this paragraph is called.

(iv) Reformed Epistemology

In this Section another alternative basis for truth-criteria in religious *Exploration* will be developed. The Fideism we have just outlined above may well seem very unsatisfactory. There is no answer to the question why accept on faith one particular interpretation of the universe as giving a true, objective account of its character. A specific way of life founded on such an interpretation may well be attractive and illuminating, but it does not follow that this interpretation's truth-claims are correct. It also appears arbitrary in a secular culture just to opt for theism without reason or even despite reason. Again it looks quite unjustifiable in a plural society, such as is ours today, to build on one faith and to assume that one scripture alone or one supremely gives an exclusive revelation of God and the way the world is.

The alternative possibility, which we discuss in this Section, is Reformed Epistemology. This is an interpretation of Calvin and of other of the Reformers, developed by some modern philosophers, such as Alvin Plantinga and Nicholas Wolterstorff.[32] The central claim is that it is unnecessary to have proofs or arguments for God's existence. Instead it is perfectly rational to hold the belief that God exists as a *basic* belief, unsubstantiated or justified by further reasons. Provided any serious objections to this belief in God are seriously considered and answered to the believers' satisfaction, they can with integrity assume theism. Beliefs, especially basic beliefs, are held to be innocent until proved guilty.[33] We are permitted to accept them, if we wish, until some criticism 'defeats' them!

The need to have arguments for God's existence is criticised as dependent on 'Foundationalism'. This is a widespread conviction in modern philosophy since Locke and Hume that all beliefs must be supported by *basic* beliefs of a certain kind or must be basic beliefs themselves. These basic beliefs have to be self-evident or incorrigible – that is, not open to correction by subsequent experience – like the truths of logic or propositions of immediate sense experience e.g. the sum of the angles of a triangle is equal to two right angles or the appearing to oneself of a coloured patch is such and such.[34] Foundationalism has been falling from favour in recent philosophy.[35] There are too many unresolved problems with sense perception and the common sense conviction we all have about the reality of physical objects. Often foundational beliefs themselves depend on others in particular contexts, like those specifying the conditions of observation when sense perception is thought to be objective.

Self-evidence and incorrigibility are also problematic and difficult notions. Moreover the central belief of Foundationalism itself, that every proposition has to be derivable from basic beliefs of the prescribed varieties, or be such a basic belief itself, cannot be justified in accordance with this central belief. Such a self-referential claim is neither itself basic in the required sense nor is deducible or supportable from what is self-evident or a matter of incorrigible sense perception.[36]

It seems preferable to treat the basicality of belief as a relative notion. Some beliefs we consider basic in certain contexts, within particular social practices, relative to specific sorts of further beliefs, subject to possible criticisms being met and objections overcome. Thus the practice of perception consists, in normal conditions of observation by normal observers, in experience being taken to be what it appears to be and conceptualised as physical objects. The principle of the practice that physical objects independently exist is assumed as a basic belief rational to hold. For in real life there is no sane alternative.

This approach is reinforced by other realms of objective knowledge where parallel practices are found with their own principles of ontology that constitute our basic beliefs.[37] Such beliefs comprise the existence of other minds, postulated to explain the mental phenomena displayed by living human bodies and affording criteria for ascribing mental predicates to people. There is the validity of testimony by which our knowledge of the world is extended beyond the narrow confines of one's personal experience and we accept truths yielded about distant times and places. Then there is the existence of the past on the strength of the memory of self and others, with further evidence for previous times being interpreted accordingly. Clearly we have no inductive proof of memory or of testimony that can proceed without circularity and assuming what is at issue, namely knowledge of the existence of things and happenings distant in space and time from the here and now.

Reformed Epistemology argues there is a parallel with God's existence as a basic belief, provided objections like the problem of evil and of undeserved suffering can be satisfactorily tackled. God's existence then becomes the principle by which everyday phenomena are redescribed in terms of God. Calvin claimed God gives an irresistible disposition to every human being to interpret the beauties of nature as God's handiwork; our sense of the moral law as his will; experiences of peace, freedom or succour as cases of forgiveness, blessing and grace etc.[38] Such experiences so conceptualised nourish belief in God and make us familiar with and proficient in religious language (and thus become other forms of our *Nourishing the Sense of God Stage*).[39] These experiences also count on particular occasions as grounds (but not as proofs) for the belief that God exists.[40] For every claim about God's activity in the world or towards believers implies and presupposes his existence.

The crucial question now is whether this analogy holds between belief in other minds, sense perception, testimony and the past as basic and between belief in God as equally basic. Clearly we have universal social practices of ascribing mental properties to minds, sensory to bodies and of relying on knowledge of the past and of distant places. Such practices are essential to human welfare and a rational existence and are central to common sense and sanity. Is the same true of the religious practice of conceptualising everyday experience in terms of God and of treating his existence as a basic belief?

The objection might run that in a secular age many people do not have an awareness of God and do not use this religious practice (or Christian Practice as Alston calls it)[41] to make sense of their lives. Not to be religious is no threat to sanity and unbelief can cope perfectly well with everyday existence.

The believer can reply that theism has been virtually universal in the past in most human societies and cultures and is still prevalent in much of the world. Certainly there is today a substantial amount of religious experience to be found.[42] So there is a considerable minority of the population who are religious and who want to live their lives in the light of the basic assumption that God exists. Why should not this postulate be a sensible choice for them? If theists can deal with Freudian, Marxist and other objections to the genuineness of religious experience[43] and can produce prima facie satisfactory arguments over the problem of evil, why should they not adopt a religious practice as a rational way to live?

In his or her existential and subjective *Exploration* of religion the follower of a faith may be attracted to the lives and examples of the religious giants of mankind like Jesus, Moses and Muhammad; St Paul, St Francis, Catherine of Genoa, Julian of Norwich, al-Hallaj, Ramanuja, Guru Nanak; and the saints of our own day, Mother Theresa, Martin Luther King, Mahatma Gandhi – all of whom have had a vivid and enduring sense of being in the presence of God. And there are the multitudes of ordinary religious people who, either from their upbringing onwards or from their conversion, find echoes in their own experience of this sense of an abiding or episodic divine presence, which is no mere redescription of sensory awareness after Calvin's fashion.

Nor is it altogether surprising that only a minority believe in God, given the powerful secular pressures of the modern world. God and the realm of the spirit are inevitably mysterious, elusive, and hard to grasp easily and readily. To come by an awareness of God may take years of practising self-discipline, denial and developing a positive will to embrace him. Nor will this area of spiritual consciousness yield simple laws and forecasts like those of science and of common sense empirical prediction, but it is none the worse for that, given the nature of its subject matter.[44]

This debate about the analogy between the widespread belief that God exists and the universal acceptance of other minds, physical objects, the past and of testimony being reliable, can continue indefinitely and perhaps will remain inconclusive. Maybe what might sway the issue would be a more modest use of natural theology. However arguments such as those in Chapter 5 **(iv)** are assessed, it is clear that they at least show the possibility that God exists and that, as Hick says,[45] this is an important possibility, opening up a whole new potential dimension of experience to which human life can be directed. Objections claiming that only a naturalistic or physicalistic account of reality is acceptable, are defeated by this modest use of natural theology. Because of this conclusion, and of Reformed Epistemology's revised ethic of belief, it does seem eminently rational to hold God's existence as a basic belief, enabling those who so wish to conceptualise ordinary experience in theistic terms. For these people are permitted to retain this basic belief, since it continues to be innocent with its 'defeaters' of evil and materialism being themselves defeated. Belief in God's existence is almost as central to these persons' epistemic structure as belief in other minds, physical objects, the past and the testimony of others. Thus there does seem to be a good prima facie case for Reformed Epistemology and we may now ask whether it affords an alternative basis for our religious truth-criteria.

Adopting Reformed Epistemology seems no reason to alter our 'Pre-Religious: logical, moral and historical' criteria. Equally we can continue to use 'philosophical argument', as its power in justifying religious belief and in discriminating what is acceptable has already been seen in Chapter **5 (iv)** and in this Section. The 'Inter-Religious' criteria of 'unopposed attestation' and of 'accommodation' clearly both depend on the foundation-teaching of the great faiths together and severally being held to disclose truth about God. This is the crucial assumption behind our 'foundational' criterion, and our key question now becomes can this premiss be justified in terms of Reformed Epistemology?

Three arguments were employed earlier in Section **(iv)** to show that God has disclosed himself in the original teachings of the great religions. How do these three reasons fare in the light of Reformed Epistemology? The first argument claims God wants intelligent creatures to know his nature and purposes and will not therefore allow great deposits of teaching about himself to evolve in a way that is grossly misleading and wrong. If we now say, however, that it *is* rational to hold an unproven belief that God exists and that such a God will want to reveal himself, the same conclusion follows. If God has any providential control over the course of events, he will ensure that the vast variety of reports about himself will not as a whole be misleading in their global upshot.

The second argument claims that religious teachers, founders of faiths and prophets are like travellers from a distant shore. Their testimony is the more rational to accept if part of it, creation, can be corroborated by the conclusion of natural theology that the world is created. Now clearly the mere possibility of there being a creator, important though that is, is not enough to support the travellers' tales. Instead we appeal to Swinburne's 'Principle of Testimony', which gives weight to the testimony of others, so long as it is reasonable in itself and they are not discredited.[46] Just as it is rational to believe without proof that God exists, so all accept in any case the rationality of testimony. But does this apply to witnesses to the transcendental realm which goes far beyond the limits of earthly spaces or planetary times. Here the more modest finding of natural theology that God may exist, and the rationality of holding God exists as a basic tenet in our epistemic structure, can meet the difficulty. If it is rational to believe in a God, who wants to be known, as we have found in the revised version of our first argument for revelation, then it is equally rational to accept the testimony of those claiming to be his messengers. A priori we may argue such a God will not permit all of these to be deceivers.

The third argument is a development from the argument from religious experience to God's existence and a corollary to this argument. The experience of seers and mystics is often coupled with teaching about God, and it is reasonable to accept that these deliverances come from the same sources which give support to our conviction of God's existence. Now it is important to recall that this variety of religious experience is on a par with sense perception, as apprehending (a) distinctive object(s), and is not to be confused with mere redescription of everyday sense experience. Those who have this distinct religious awareness claim to perceive God, and by the 'Principle of Credulity',[47] if there is no further objection, their testimony may be accepted. On the premisses of Reformed Epistemology this type of quasi-perceptual apprehension of God can be still taken to be what it claims to be, if God's existence is held as a basic belief and criticisms to this belief can be defeated. This is in just the same way that the redescription of ordinary sense experience in terms of God, Calvin's triggers of the divine, which are instinctive in traditionally brought-up people, can be also accepted as objective. Hence when seers and mystics claim to teach *about* God, deriving what they offer from their consciousness of him making himself known to them, what they teach can be regarded as revelation, for those whose belief in God's existence is basic.

Thus our three arguments for the identification of revelation in the foundation-teachings of the great faiths can be maintained on the basis of Reformed Epistemology, supplemented by natural theology employed in a modest, innocuous and subordinate way. So our 'foundational' criterion, the linchpin of our set of criteria for religious truth, can be properly used in *Exploration* by the Communicatee under the guidance of the Communicator.

(v) The Stage of Commitment

In *Exploration* the ideal explorer will apply the 'pre-religious', the 'intra-religious' and the 'inter-religious' truth-criteria to the material he or she has come to know in the Stage of *Learning*. They may well end up as sceptical or agnostic or, alternatively, as believing the claims found in the ruling conception of what it is to be a Christian (or of some other faith). Should the Communicatee regard the Christian beliefs as plausible enough for rational, if tentative assent, he or she may move on to the last Stage, the Stage of *Commitment*. It should be unnecessary at this point to remind the reader that we have only been sketching an ideal explorer's voyage across the oceans of philosophical theology. Few will go the whole way or need to. How far any actual Communicatee's quest approximates to the ideal will depend on the multitude of ad hoc qualifications considered above. But it is worth remembering that any pupil, child, student, potential convert or mature Christian may well at any point raise questions of religious truth which, we claim, can only be rationally answered by trying to apply one or more of our criteria

What kind of *Commitment* is appropriate as the content of the last stage in our Theory of Religious Communication? The answer will vary according to the several communicative activities distinguished.[48]

Evangelism and *Child Nurture* intend to bring about ultimately an autonomous, substantive commitment to the Christian (or other theistic) faith. This is why a further Stage of *Commitment* is needed beyond that of *Exploration*. On the basis of a tentative and cautious decision that the main claims of Christianity (or some other faith) are true, even if they are held with a considerable measure of agnosticism, a person is properly free to commit him or herself to living a Christian life according to the ruling conception learnt of what it is to be a Christian (or to allow the drift of his or her thinking, maybe aided, some would claim, by divine grace, to bring the Communicatee to living faith). The Communicatee is able to make with a good conscience the vows demanded at Baptism or Confirmation, or to begin to live as a committed believer, if they are already a member of the community by Infant Baptism.

Of course as a result of *Exploration* the Communicatee may finish up an unbeliever or largely agnostic. Or he or she may embrace some of the beliefs of one faith, some of another or of several others, in an idiosyncratic syncretistic pattern. Whether commitment to any particular religion is then morally possible with integrity will be a matter of pastoral guidance on the part of the Communicator. Maybe there can be a commitment to another faith than the one the Communicator has set out from at the beginning of the process; maybe some avowal of one faith in a very liberal form far distant from orthodoxy, perhaps with some admixture of the tenets of a different religion, will be a proper position to attain in Stage VIII. In the end the only commitment allowable could be the educational one to continue exploration: and such a termination of the process cannot be regarded as an entire failure by a Communicator with liberal values!

The transition from a tentative adherence to Christian truth (or to that of some other faith) to a mature, permanent and deep commitment occurs when Christianity becomes an existential choice of a way of life. This is characteristically and normatively embraced as a whole and held in a way resistant to endless overthrow by the minor objections and the numerous difficulties which we cannot always overcome as we live our lives. To make something of a Christian identity and life-style, faith needs thorough testing and trial over time, giving it the benefit of the doubt, not easily giving up, as in the comparable commitment of marriage.[49] Of course, this is not to say that further reflection is not permissible or desirable, or even obligatory, but the commitment we are concerned with is a serious moral choice, appropriate if the Gospel's truth-claims are accepted, though naturally this choice is not necessarily demanded. Belief without faith is quite possible: for the devils also believe and tremble![50]

Inter-Faith Dialogue proceeds between committed believers. Experience suggest that beliefs will not change sufficiently through mutual exploration of each other's position to permit any substantial alteration of commitment away from or towards another faith. However, the dialogist's commitment may be modified, becoming less dogmatic and more sympathetic through a greater understanding of his or her colleague's belief-system. Indeed *Exploration* could result in the adherent of one faith accepting some of the beliefs of the other religionist he or she has been dialoguing with. A Christian may come to believe the prophet Muhammad is indeed on a par with Moses or Elijah, and a Jew similarly. A Muslim could perhaps realise that what the Qur'an says about Issa, that he (as a Muslim) thought Christians wrongly believed, is not in fact what the Creeds teach. Western theists may realise that

Nirvana or Brahman or Sunyata may at bottom refer to something in the divine mysteries and Hindus or Buddhists could come to know how the Transcendent can be thought of as ultimately personal. A believer after *Inter-Faith Dialogue* may thus find that some important elements in the treasures of another's beliefs and practice can be integrated into his or her own outlook without loss of integrity or weakening of commitment.

Nurture of adults presupposes a basic commitment to a faith and it aims to deepen and widen such commitment.[51] *Nurture* may involve strengthening the original *Commitment* by further *Learning* or *Exploration* or it may involve making fresh commitments to particular aspects or practices of a religion. Nurturing can lead to accepting a specific vocation to some form or style of living within the Christian life and to becoming committed to this. And, of course, in theory if the exploratory phases of *Nurture* result in unbelief, at this Stage commitment may have to be re-evaluated.

For *Religious Education* and the *Academic Study of a Religion,* aiming by the teacher at substantive commitment to a faith or to an unbelieving position at the end of the process, is inappropriate and indeed ruled out by the nature of these public, communicative enterprises, concerned with controversial subject-matter and operating within a pluralist, secular society.[52] (In actual fact, however, substantive commitment on the part of the Communicator and Communicatee is not precluded at either the beginning or the finish of the course: otherwise committed believers could not take part in these activities!) But it is important to realise, nonetheless, that *Religious Education* and *Academic Study* should aim at a commitment on the part of pupils and students to the general academic values of truth, relevance, accuracy and impartiality in examining disputed matters. With regard to religion, teachers should try to encourage commitment to the quest to explore thoroughly, carefully and persistently. The Stage of *Exploration* does not end when young people leave school or college but should continue in later life: permanent disposition to search and reflect on these issues should be part of the commitment that being educated entails.

What variety of commitment does *Ministerial Formation* aim at? In so far as it is a form of *Nurture* its appropriate objective will be to deepen a pre-existing, positive and substantive commitment to the Communicatee's faith, in particular that to a special vocation, like being a minister. When, however, *Ministerial Formation* overlaps with Higher Education, its end-product should be the same as that of the *Academic Study of Religion,* namely an educational commitment to academic values, especially those relevant to controversy and to the endless pursuit of truth.

These two objectives of the combined aspects of study and nurture that comprise *Ministerial Formation* are entirely compatible. Christian and other faith commitment, especially to a professional religious vocation, should certainly include dedication to academic values. Commitment to a faith must surely rest on the positive outcome of a search for truth that can continue lifelong, since ongoing *Nurture* is a permanent requirement in a minister. But, if further exploration leads to unbelief, then, as we have seen above with *Nurture* in general, a difficult revision of faith commitment may be demanded by integrity. There is no special problem here for *Ministerial Formation* (though there may be agonising personal and pastoral decisions to make): with any of our species of religious communication there is the risk that in a controversial area the outcome may be the loss of faith of any substantive particular variety.

What part may the Communicator play in this last Stage? With *Evangelism, Child Nurture* and the *Nurture* of adults, the Communicator should seek substantive commitment and employ all proper means of teaching, preaching, exhortation, encouragement and counselling. What this involves in detail depends on the age, outlook and circumstances of the Communicatee. With *Inter-Faith Dialogue* no new points arise, since the dialogists are both Communicator and Communicatee. With *Religious Education* and *Academic Study* the teacher's public intention follows from the kind of commitment appropriate to these activities. In the course of discussion with pupils and students the teacher may, by precept and example, make the case for the commitment to explore and to the values implicit in the search. The Communicator should go further and try to convert the pupil's or student's conviction of the importance of truth or of exploration into a passion for truth and exploration.[53] Thus will be generated the affective aspect of the quest that is necessary if the Communicatee is actually to do and to keep on doing what he or she ought, despite contrary feelings, temptation and pressures.

If the teacher of *Religious Education* or *Academic Study* is also a committed Christian, they may hope and pray in private that pupils and students may come to substantive Christian commitment and they will be ready to help pastorally the Communicatee who decides to make such a commitment (and so for other faiths where appropriate). But the Communicator's professionalism as a teacher at the very least demands he or she is careful that their private beliefs do not distort or disturb their public practice and make them less impartial and objective when stimulating the Communicatee to learn and to explore.

Thus we conclude our examination of *Learning* what it is to be an adherent of a faith; of *Exploring* both existentially and in terms of truth-criteria a theistic religion; and of the kinds of *Commitment* sought after in the various species of religious communication. We now reach the end of expounding our Stage Theory of Religious Communication. It remains to discuss the Theory's practical application, objections to it, and training for Communicators, and to present our concluding vision.

Notes

1. v. **1** (iii)
2. v. **5** (ii)
3. v. **3** (ii)
4. Kelly, J. N. D. (1950*), Early Christian Creeds,* Longmans, London, 296–368.
5. Attfield, D. G. (1976), A Taxonomy of Religious Concepts, *Learning for Living,* **16:2,** 68–75.
6. v. **4** (i).
7. v. **3** (i).
8. For a useful analysis v. Astley, J. (1994), The Place of understanding in Christian Education and education about Christianity, **2.4**, in Astley, J. and Francis, L. J., *Critical Perspectives in Christian Education,* Gracewing, Leominster.
9. Astley, (1994) op. cit.,235–241.
10. Thiessen, op. cit.,
11. v. **1** (20) and (21).
12. Matthew *16:26* = Mark *8:36* = Luke *9:25.*
13. *Pensées,* (E. T.) Stewart, H. F. (1950), Routledge and Kegan Paul, London, §223, 115–123.
14. Freeman, A., *God in Us,* (1993), S. C. M. Press, London, **1** and **2**; Cupitt, D. (1980), *Taking Leave of God,* S. C. M. Press, London,**1**– **4**.
15. Cf. Hebblethwaite, B. (1980), *The Problems of Theology,* C. U. P., Cambridge, 38–43.
16. Op. cit., 76–78.
17. Ibid., 68–76; Cf. Barbour, I. (1990), *Religion in an Age of Science,* S. C. M. Press, London, 34.
18. Hobson and Edwards, op. cit., 38–40, 80–82.
19. Section (iii).
20. Flew, A. G. N. and MacIntyre, A. C. (1955), *New Essays in Philosophical Theology,* S. C. M. Press, London, 96–130.
21. Astley (1994), op. cit.,262–289; McIntyre, M. (1988), *Whose Justice? Which Rationality?,* Duckworth, London and Notre Dame University Press, Notre Dame, **18,19,20**.
22. Swinburne, R. (1970), *The Concept of Miracles,* Macmillan, London, **6**.
23. v. **4** (18). v. **5** (iv) on the Reality of God for a concise example, the comparable Section (iv) in this Chapter on Reformed Epistemology and the immediately following discussion deployed in support of our foundational criteria.
24. Swinburne, R. (1992), *Revelation,* Clarendon Press, Oxford, **5**; Lonergan, B. F. J. (1958), *Insight,* Harper Row, New York, 687–703,718–730.
25. v. **5** (iv).
26. Lewis, op. cit.,**2, 3, 5, 6, 8**.
27. Qur'an, s. 5.
28. Ibid., ss. 2,10,19.
29. Ibid., ss. 5, 9, 23, 112.
30. Smart, N. (1960), *A Dialogue of Religions,* S. C. M. Press, London, **4**. For a valiant attempt at 'Accommodation', c.f. Kung H., (1993), *Christianity and World Religions,* 2nd Ed. S. C. M. Press, London, 208–209, 393–398. C.f. also Hick, J., (1989), *An Interpretation of Religion,* Macmillan, London, **14, 15, 16.**
31. Ibid., 287–292.
32. Helm, P. (1997), *Faith and Understanding,* Edinburgh University Press, Edinburgh, **8**; Morris, T. V. Ed. (1994), *God and the Philosophers,* 92–99,197–205, 267–270; Plantinga,

A. and Wolterstorff, N. (1983), *Faith and Rationality,* University of Notre Dame Press, London.

[33] Wolterstorff in Platinga and Wolterstorff, op. cit., 162–178.
[34] Plantinga in ibid.,47–59.
[35] Ibid., 59 ff.
[36] Ibid.,59–63.
[37] Ibid.,79–82.
[38] Ibid., 65–68.
[39] v. **5** (ii).
[40] Ibid., 78–82.
[41] Alston in ibid.,110–113.
[42] v. **5** (8).
[43] v. **5** (30).
[44] Alston in ibid.,128–133.
[45] Op. cit., 219.
[46] Op cit.,(1979), 271–274.
[47] v. **5** (iv).
[48] v. **1** (iii).
[49] Mitchell (1973) op. cit., **7**; (1994) op. cit.,**1–3**; cf. also Levinson, op. cit., on the relation of long term commitment to autonomy, 32–34; Morris, op. cit.,199–202.
[50] James 2:19.
[51] v. **1** (iii).
[52] v. **1** (iv).
[53] Peters, R. S. (1972), Reason and Passion, in Dearden, R. F., Hirst, P. H. and Peters, R. S. Eds. *Education and the Development of Reason,* Routledge and Kegan Paul, London, **12**; (1973), *Reason and Compassion*, Routledge and Kegan Paul, London, **3**.

Chapter 8

Application

In this Chapter we shall draw together the threads of our argument by applying our Stage Theory of Religious Communication in turn to each of the communicative activities we have distinguished.[1] A strategy for each activity will be outlined and the practical application of our analysis will be suggested. (Our examples will all be Christian; those of other faiths can work out their own equivalents.)

(i) Evangelism

We assume that *Evangelism* should be a routine, regular and normal activity of a local church. At its heart is what in this Chapter we shall now term 'evangelism proper'. This activity makes provision for our stages of *Learning, Exploration* and *Commitment* e.g. Alpha Courses, Emmaus Courses or the Gospel Down The Street;[2] these courses embrace exposition of Christianity, enabling *Learning* and supporting *Exploration* by discussion, and at some point presenting a challenge to *Commitment*.

What is not obvious is whatever is needed to meet the requirements of our earlier Stages, since churches are not in general aware of the necessity for them to prepare for 'evangelism proper'. These preliminaries to Evangelism proper we call 'preparation for evangelism'. This we divide into 'early and later preparation'. 'Early preparation' affects the Communicatee years before 'evangelism proper'; 'later preparation' takes place a few years or months before a particular exercise in 'evangelism proper'.

Early preparation comprises some of our Background Conditions and elements in *Nourishing the Sense of God*. This early preparation occurs in childhood in home or school or both. A local church participates in early preparation in so far as it can influence child-rearing and education. In the first place home and school cultivate *Verbal Ability* (which may also be developed in Youth Work, Training of the Unemployed and Adult Literacy projects, all of which can be supported and encouraged by local churches).[3]

Secondly and similarly, *Autonomy* may be promoted in upbringing and schooling, either being positively encouraged or at least not being prevented: nothing should be done that hinders the growth of independence of mind, self-control and competence. In theory these are generated spontaneously by the socialisation of children in modern society, an ideal the church should uphold in the local situation. (The Background Condition of *Opportunity* will be considered later.)

Thirdly a child's *Sense of God* may be *Nourished* in school *Religious Education* and worship, by presenting the concept of God as a person, creator and object of worship, as much in Community as in Voluntary (State) schools.[4] Again church involvement in education, wherever it can be exercised, is of critical importance. Also there is the direct influence of the church on worshippers, who only attend church occasionally, over the years prior to their encountering evangelism proper. In all these ways, early preparation makes possible the receiving of the religious message.

As well as early preparation, later preparation for evangelism proper is also needed as part of an ideal church strategy for *Evangelism*. Later preparation has two aspects which have to be in place in the activity of the same persons or groups in the local church. Firstly the crucial task, as 'evangelism proper' approaches, is to *Nourish* the Communicatee's *Sense of God* through the witness of ordinary Christians. By the witness of their love, by what they say and do, and above all by what they are, they become people who are transparent to God; and then in the Communicatee awareness of the idea of God and a sense of the importance of his claims on us are deepened and intensified.

Now, secondly, at the same time and by the same Communicators, the Communicatees have to become initiated into church-associated activities to facilitate *Motivation*. According to taste and temperament, as analysed in Chapter 5 on personality types, following the Myers-Briggs' classificatory scheme,[5] the Communicatee comes to share in various activities with Christians. Either these activities can be run by the church itself or they may be activities of the local community, provided a significant minority of Christians is active in each enterprise and can properly have an high profile in it. It is the combination of church-related activity, on the part of those who are ignorant of or unbelieving in the faith, with their newly engendered *Sense of God*, that will produce the cognitive dissonance, motivating these Communicatees to want to find out more about Christianity. The Communicatee is brought towards the Gospel by a common, secular interest shared with the Christian, the very same person who has witnessed to him or her that God is real: friendship and witness together are the secret of *Motivation*.

The final step in the evangelistic strategy of the local church is for it to take account of *Opportunity*: thought must be consciously given about plans, dates, times of offering evangelism proper, in relation to the circumstances of the Communicatee (thus the third Background Condition is allowed for). Then when early and later preparation is complete, our earlier stages are satisfied and the Communicatee will want to learn and to explore and will be willing seriously to consider *Commitment*. Notice that early and later preparation and evangelism proper are particular enterprises, quite independent of each other, and are best conceived as parts of the normal ongoing life of a local church. Success depends on persistence over time and as much energy being invested in the earlier as in the later Stages of the total communicative activity of *Evangelism*.

As well as a local church strategy for *Evangelism*, every Christian in their witnessing and every evangelist in approaching people, needs a strategy. For this purpose our Theory provides a diagnostic tool. Estimate what Stage the Communicatee has reached and then you know where to begin. According to Communicatee's current condition, it may be best to concentrate on V*erbal Ability* or *Autonomy* or on *Nurturing their Sense of God*. If they are becoming motivated, then it is time to seek O*pportunity* and to plan *Learning*. On the extent and quality of *Learning*, the Communicator must decide whether to encourage *Exploration*. Those who 'preach for a verdict', or who press 'decision' and urge faith, must be sure the Communicatee is ready, having autonomously come to believe: and can now properly proceed to *Commitment*.

(ii) Inter-Faith Dialogue

Inter-Faith Dialogue is next considered as a special application of our Theory, in the light of the treatment just given to *Evangelism*. In recent years a consensus has emerged that *Inter-Faith Dialogue* is the proper form witness and faith-sharing take, when Christianity meets other faiths and vice versa.[6] In terms of our Theory we shall argue that Dialogue is the only appropriate form *Evangelism* can assume with a Communicatee who already has a rich and complex religious commitment of his or her own, other than that which the Communicator wants to pass on. Thus it will also follow that the same kind of *Evangelism* should be employed towards a Marxist, Humanist or advocate of any other non-religious philosophy or world-view (however, in our discussion, such a dialogue with secular faiths will not be pursued).

It has come to be agreed that *Inter-Faith Dialogue* should be conducted in accordance with the well-known British Council of Churches' Guidelines.[7] These are four:

I 'Dialogue begins when people meet each other.'
In Dialogue one deals with an actual person of flesh and blood, a concrete individual with their own interpretation and experience of a religion, not with a belief-system in the abstract, nor a dialogist as a mere standard, impersonal representative of a faith.[8]

II 'Dialogue depends on mutual understanding and mutual trust.'
Nothing should be done to threaten the other person, to misrepresent their position or to display prejudice. On the contrary, trust has to be built up in the context of what becomes a personal friendship.

III 'Dialogue makes it possible to share in service to the community.'
Before the sensitive ground of religious difference is reached, the common service of humanity will cement the relationship and prepare the way for dialogue. The participants become aware of how much they can share in meeting human need together, in virtue of the different faiths they hold.

IV 'Dialogue becomes the medium of authentic witness.'
The dialogists witness to each other. There is mutual learning and exploration, leading first to enhanced understanding of the other's faith and then to the enrichment of their own. Such a meeting of minds is not without risk.[9] L. Newbigin claims, 'A dialogue which is safe from all possible risks is no true dialogue'.[10] Either dialogist may have to follow the truth wherever it leads them and modify their own position. In principle, conversion is not impossible!

How may our Theory be applied to illuminate what is involved in Dialogue? At the outset it should be noted that in our terminology the Christian will first be the Communicator and the person of other faith the Communicatee. In fact, though, because of the nature of Dialogue, each communicates with the other, so *both* take *both* roles in turn, the Christian being as much Communicatee as Communicator. So we consider our Stages one by one and in order.

That there is *Verbal Ability* sufficient for the purposes of Dialogue can be assumed. Both parties will not reach the level of Dialogue unless they are relatively well-informed, educated adherents of their faiths and so will have what is needed for debate.

Some autonomy may also be taken for granted on the part of the dialogists, so their faith may change as they proceed. But it is quite possible that the Communicatee may come from a religion and culture where autonomy is not prized. His or her lack of it might make modification of their own commitment difficult, as the process unfolds. Probably they can move more easily in discussion than in spiritual position. In the course of time, however, the effect of modern education on the dialogists of the future will be to enhance autonomy and so to aid communication.

From the fact that Dialogue is possible and practical for given people to pursue, it follows that *Opportunity* is available. What this *Opportunity* condition may do is to restrict Dialogue to those who have the leisure, energy and enough freedom from other commitments to undertake this time-consuming exercise! Advocates of Dialogue may care to reflect how far each of our Background Conditions tends to make Dialogue unrepresentative of ordinary believers.

Our Stages that concern *Motivation* and *Nourishing the Sense of God* generate motivation by non-religious association with the church on the part of those with an intensified idea of God: these conditions may be, however, assumed to be satisfied in any Dialogue. The participants we are dealing with are committed believers to whom God (or the Ultimate in non-theistic faiths) is very real and is taken most seriously. They are well motivated also for *Learning* and *Exploration*. Otherwise they would not enter Dialogue. It may well also be the case that the developing friendship between the dialogists and their joint servicing of human need may reinforce their religious motivation to proceed more directly with their conversation.

The Stage of *Learning* presents problems for the application of our Theory to Dialogue. The dialogists are concrete believers, explaining their personal faith and witnessing to their personal experience, and are not mere holders of the standard content of a given belief-system, exponents of what we have called the 'ruling-conception' of a faith. What the content of *Learning* now becomes is what constitutes the identity of the concrete believer in dialogue. This may diverge widely from the standard teaching of an historical religion, though not so far from the ruling-concept as to invalidate the claim of the dialogist to represent his or her faith. An unnoticed presupposition of Dialogue is that the partners are relatively orthodox adherents of their religion: otherwise this encounter will not qualify as properly Inter-Faith between the faiths concerned and will not advance mutual understanding between such belief-systems, on the part of ordinary upholders of them.

Our Stage of *Exploration* lies at the heart of the mutual witness in a Dialogue. If this is to proceed profitably, both partners must be at one on which of our two interpretations of exploration they are working with. Do they agree that religion is a matter of objective truth or is it just a question of personal preference? Do they sufficiently acknowledge the underlying criteria they apply? A philosophical understanding in the background needs to be clear, even if not explicitly formulated, for actual *Exploration* is probably ad hoc and not systematic. It is, however, quite possible that this philosophical background is not held in common. Then, difficult as the exercise may be, the most useful and hopeful form of dialogue is a mutual *Exploration* of the dialogists' presuppositions with the object of charting the exact contours of agreement and disagreement.

Our last Stage of *Commitment* hardly applies in any direct way to Dialogue. The usual intention of the participants is mutual understanding and *Exploration.* Unlike *Evangelism*, where the intention is to convert (or equivalent),[11] in Dialogue the partners stop at the intention to witness and to share their faith. The absence of an intention to convert in the Christian dialogist is partly because, if they were to admit to such an intent, the other dialogist would be frightened off and the dialogue would be destroyed. Also, in view of the unhappy past history of Christian relations with other faiths and the empirical fact of the rarity of conversions from other religions, an evangelistic intention is just not a sensible one to have. Nonetheless it should be noted that change of commitment is in principle possible through Dialogue, if not very likely at this stage in the history of faith-sharing, and may be an incidental result of this process.

Thus we maintain that *Inter-Faith Dialogue* is clarified by and comprehended in our Stage Theory, which casts considerable light on what is being attempted in this important new practice.

(iii) Nurture of Adults

Every local church needs a strategy for *Nurture,* as much as for *Evangelism.* The Christian community can proceed on roughly similar lines to those of having an 'early' and 'later preparation' for 'evangelism proper'. 'Early preparation' for 'nurture proper, begins years back. *Nurture* of adult committed Christians is much more likely to be profitable if their *Verbal Ability* and *Autonomy* have been developed. It should be noticed that church life itself provides for these *Background Conditions*. Worship and public prayer are conducted in words, obviously appropriate words for expressing faith, and thus committed and practising Christians gradually become familiar with the language of religion and capable of employing it. Again sharing in church activity in terms of discussion and committee work will foster autonomy in a church where lay ministry is welcomed.

It might be thought that committed Christians are highly motivated to learn and to explore more deeply their own faith. Sadly this is not necessarily so and often congregations will do no more than attend services more or less regularly, though worship itself should nurture those present (albeit this is not its main purpose). So 'later preparation' for nurture proper, *Nourishing the Sense of God* and *Motivation* of committed Christians, according to type, are needed. It is to be hoped that exposure to worship and prayer over the years *Nourish* their *Sense of God*. Committed believers may also be willing to meditate upon their own contingency, our fourth form of such nourishment. Again, participation in church life, of whatever kind, that interests and involves the congregation, may engender such attachment to the church as an organisation that, in conjunction with an aroused awareness of God, worshippers will come to feel a pressure to know more and to explore.

When the Communicatee is sufficiently motivated, nurturing courses or other varieties of *Nurture* can now be profitably arranged. In doing this, when planning nurturant activities, account should be taken of the circumstances of Christians' lives, so that *Opportunity* may be offered in a form and at a time that is convenient and practicable. Such programmes of nurture proper that may be arranged by the local (or regional or national) church should be of a wide variety to meet the many and varying needs of committed Christians of all abilities at every age and stage of their lives. Chances for appropriate *Learning, Exploration* and further *Commitment,* such as to taking a leadership role in the church, can then be provided. Again it is important to underline the use of our Theory as a diagnostic tool in estimating where the Communicatee is and what is the next appropriate step for him or her.

With advanced forms of *Nurture*, a particular problem may arise. *Nurture* presupposes commitment and yet commitment itself may be threatened if *Exploration* leads to fundamental beliefs of the Communicatee being undermined. In the short run there will be no problem here because it is psychologically possible to hold conflicting beliefs at the same time. Pressures of argument and evidence on the one hand may incline Communicatees to abandon their basic creed or at least to think it may be false. On the other hand they will continue to hold such tenets of their religion as a 'matter of faith' i.e. beliefs unsupported now by any reasons or by inadequate reasons. And the practical implications for religious practice of such faith in God or in Christ, in terms of trust in and obedience to the objects of this belief, will be sustained by this bare conviction, since it is a question of 'belief in' and not just 'belief that'. Moreover the further commitments taken on by baptism, confirmation or ordination vows will remain in force.

The hope of the nurturer is of course that rational support for faith will in due course return as thinking proceeds further during the process of *Exploration*. The intention is that faith to be strengthened must be put at risk and go through the full fires of criticism, so that believers can confidently face the challenges the modern world will subsequently make to their basic belief.

We have already noted what happens if rational foundation for faith is not reconstructed after a while. Communicatees may opt for Fideism and continue to believe without grounds or despite insuperable objection. At least they are then self-aware and conscious of their position with its limits and drawbacks. Alternatively integrity and personal consistency may demand the surrender of faith and its inherent element of commitment. Additional commitment made by vows will have no force, once the beliefs that warrant such promising are no longer held. Agonising as loss of faith is for the believer, the Communicator's residual pastoral responsibility is to ease the path of the Communicatee out of the faith-community, for as long as honesty requires agnosticism.

(iv) Child Nurture

It has been argued earlier that children within the church should be nurtured towards autonomous commitment at the threshold of adult life. A programme of teaching, comparable to *Religious Education*, adjusted to the age and ability of the child, ought to extend throughout childhood in the context of worship. The Communicatee in this case will most likely be a Christian by baptism in infancy, and a practising Christian by sharing regularly in worship.

As we have claimed above with *Evangelism* and *Nurture* (adult), the Background Conditions of *Verbal Ability* and *Autonomy* should be the concerns of the local church, largely to be realised in home and school with the support and encouragement of the Christian community. The church's own worship and nurturing activity, however, should reinforce *Verbal Ability* and *Autonomy*, giving opportunity to exercise them at every point. Attendance at services and at church organisations should provide the *Opportunity* needed, taking account of the busy lives and many secular commitments of young people nowadays.

The example of older worshippers, their witness and the power of the liturgy itself, will *Nourish* young people's *Sense of God*. Their *Motivation* to learn and to explore further should be furnished by the varied, attractive activities, which a church and its youth-organisations offer young folk who are coming to see that God is real, important and exciting.

A graduated programme of religious or Christian education (to use the U.S. Protestant term) will present the ruling conception of Christianity in its several dimensions in a spiral curriculum that winds up the age-scale, as children grow into maturity. At first Christian belief will come over as what *we* believe is the case – and indeed it *is*! – then what *Christians*, but not others believe – and what *may* be the case! As young people grow into adolescence, corresponding to the Secondary phase of schooling, the emphasis becomes one of standing-back from what they have been brought up in and of appraising it critically. Other faiths enter the Christian *Nurture* of children as models for comparison with the Gospel. Present commitment should be *discouraged* until adolescents are mature enough, are sufficiently well-informed, and have explored the issues involved to a point when they can evaluate their childhood faith as rational beings. Then young adults, as they are by now, can make their own assent to Christian belief and move on to a *Commitment* to live by it.

In some churches, long before children reach years of discretion and suitability for mature commitment, they may in fact be encouraged to make some sort of personal commitment by being Baptised, Confirmed, becoming a Church Member, being qualified to receive Holy Communion etc. In principle, from the viewpoint of our Theory, and on the moral grounds that lie behind our reservations about premature commitment, such earlier vows or 'decisions' for faith should be deferred. In practice, because of the pressures and examples of peers and parents and others, and because of the disciplinary requirements of the various Denominations, younger adolescents may be trapped into such early and childish commitments. When this happens, the Communicator should stress that further *Exploration* is not foreclosed but must go on. It is also no disgrace for young people to change their minds about their basic beliefs and to adjust their *Commitment* accordingly: for instance, promises and vows must be seen against the background of the child's immaturity at the time he or she made them.

(v) Religious Education

Much of what has been argued above, except in the Stages of *Learning* and *Exploration*, will be familiar to the *Religious Education* teacher. In these Stages one possible deficiency in current *Religious Education* is in fulfilling its exploratory aim: S.C.A.A. Aim C expresses this in these terms, 'to develop the ability to make reasoned and informed judgements about religious and moral issues, with reference to the teachings of the principal religions represented in Great Britain'. Teachers seem quite happy to discuss moral issues but much less confident with religious ones.[12] In our Theory serious attention has been given to discussing religious truth-criteria, in assessing faiths as belief-systems or life-options. Of course, even in the Stage of *Exploration* (apart perhaps from Sixth Form work) we do not recommend any formal and systematic presentation of our truth-criteria (or of any other set), still less of their philosophical background.

Exploration in school will be almost entirely occasional, not systematic. A specific religious belief is presented, explained or alluded to; a pupil asks whether it is true or the teacher provokes such a response; in the course of discussion, the teacher, who has criteria at the back of his or her mind, will encourage debate to proceed along rational lines, seeing that relevant considerations, pro and con, are brought to bear. Some necessary account may have to be given of why this criterion is relevant and a small excursus into philosophy of religion may be desirable. But in school this will be ad hoc.

Whatever conclusion pupils come to, it is a further part of *Religious Education* to explain the nature of the logical connection of belief to commitment; the kind appropriate for students and teachers in contrast to the sort faiths demand of their adherents; also to make clear the difference between accepting a scientific hypothesis and per contra adopting a general theory in science or a life-option like marriage.[13]

Where our Theory has something extra to offer *Religious Education* is in the wider requirements of the Theory. First there is the importance of the *Background Conditions*. *Verbal Ability* and *Autonomy* are the products of a good upbringing and general education. *Religious Education*, therefore, presupposes liberal child-rearing in home and nursery and the development of literacy, oracy and powers of thought across the whole curriculum. The foundations of *Religious Education* are laid in the Primary school, especially in English: they are continued and reinforced by every kind of learning in the Secondary phase.

Opportunity is provided if the school honours the Basic Curriculum,[14] takes the relevant Agreed Syllabus seriously and allows Dearing's recommended 5% of total curriculum time to *Religious Education*,[15] especially with older pupils and those preparing for public examinations. *Opportunity* also requires, so that chances to learn are really available, proper resourcing for *Religious Education* in terms of funding equipment and subject-specialist teachers.

Our Theory further underlines how crucial motivation is to *Religious Education*. Obviously pupils must be interested if *Learning* and *Exploration* are to flourish. Natural curiosity and spontaneous enthusiasm will be generated by good teaching in the Primary phase and the early Secondary years. However, interest declines in adolescence on the part of many pupils.[16] Earlier we have argued that Church schools with a Christian foundation, ethos and example, can do something to counter the pressures of the secular environment in which young people grow up, and to *Nourish* the students' *Sense of God*.[17] It is unclear what County schools can do in this respect, except to encourage staff, pupils and others in the school-community, who are believers in any theistic faith and visitors from local faith-communities to witness to their Sense of God, in order to make *Religious Education* a viable proposition.

Motivation, associating the Communicatee with religious communities in non-religious ways, to generate cognitive dissonance, cannot be effected in *Religious Education*. Nor will the ordinary steps be effective which the teacher takes to link his or her subject-matter to the pupils' existing secular concerns by way of analogy, such as letting the pupils bring to school mementoes, family portraits, medals etc. and comparing these to the sacred artefacts of a faith. Such steps may provide a 'way in' to a topic but interest fails unless pupils also value religion and think it important – whether or not they are of any faith – because their *Sense of God* has been *Nourished*. When that is the case, cognitive dissonance may be used directly as *Motivation* in *Religious Education* by comparing the beliefs, values and prejudices of the children with tenets of a faith they now feel is significant: the values of youth and the values of the Kingdom may clash and adolescents will want to explore such a divergence.

Thus our Theory puts *Religious Education* into a wider context and reminds the teacher that *Background Conditions* and *Motivation* are crucial, as is also *Exploration*, conducted with some degree of philosophical sophistication on the professional Communicator's part.

(vi) Academic Study of Religion

In the *Academic Study of Religion* there is reason to distinguish Religious Studies from Theology. Religious Studies, where the issue of the truth of the basic claims of a faith is 'bracketed out' and which take an entirely open approach to religion by staff and students, are obviously at home in the modern, secular university in a liberal society. Theology, which in principle expounds one faith from its own foundation-teaching and from this religion's later development and which is concerned with a religion's positive truth-claims, also has a place in the same educational setting, despite the fact that, at the academic level of scholarship, research and teaching, a Department of Theology is officially neutral between religions and has no faith-commitment of its own.

Theology can play its part in such a department in two ways. *Either*, because of their professional public role, teachers of Theology may believe faith is true on proper grounds, yet without being committed to it as a living religion. As became clear in our discussion of commitment,[18] a tentative, provisional, academic assent to religious claims does not necessarily lead to personal faith. *Or* a theologian may argue on a 'for the sake of argument' basis e.g. 'granted God exists and has made himself known in the Bible, such and such follows'. These alternative intellectual foundations for theology in a secular university (as opposed to a Seminary officially committed to faith) are, of course, quite compatible with private commitment for or against a particular religion as a belief-system and way of life.

Whether *Academic Study of Religion* takes the form of Religious Studies or Theology makes no difference to the illumination our Stage Theory offers. In the first place, Higher Education takes the *Background Conditions* for granted. High entry qualifications ensure *Verbal Ability*. *Autonomy* in students is harder to assess at interview. But if *Autonomy* is not well developed, the Communicatee is unlikely to be happy or to profit from the *Academic Study of Religion*, since the subject requires not only intellectual power, but imaginative freedom to empathise with various religious positions and ways of life in turn, as work proceeds.

Once the student is selected and begins the course, one could argue that the *Opportunity* condition is satisfied. This is true, but the tightening of university- and student-funding suggests that *Opportunity* may not in the future be so readily available as in the past, especially if the *Academic Study of Religion* appears not very vocational for most students and to have little cash value.

Again it might be claimed that in Higher Education, *Motivation* can be taken for granted, like ability. Whether a student tackles Religious Studies or Theology because he or she happens to be interested in religion, or because they have a vocational interest in becoming a Minister or *Religious Education* teacher, may seem of no concern to their teacher. Yet such teachers of theology might reflect on how interest needs to be sustained over a rigorous three or four year course and that it will do their department's name no good when students' motivation fades late in their career and their work deteriorates. It is also clear that academic interest in religion is not totally different from the kind of interest that leads a Communicatee to take trouble to undertake *Learning* and *Exploration* at the much lower levels of the other species of Communication we have distinguished.

If the undergraduates' Sense of God is not deep and intense, at least they need some awareness of the importance of religion in world culture and civilisation and in understanding them.[19] Moreover the *Academic Study of Religion* wants a wider range of students than those qualified and suitable to become scholars. This discipline (or disciplines) is indeed unlikely to contribute to the wider education of undergraduates, unless they become deeply attached to their subject and its implications for living by those who adopt the faith under scrutiny.

It would seem then for these reasons that the quality of the students' motivation should be of concern to the teacher. Can he or she do much to foster interest in their subject? Academics should be glad if, in the earlier stages of the young person's life, churches, schools and other bodies have engendered curiosity about faith and interest in pursuing rigorously and in depth questions about religion. Probably in a department some students and some of the faculty have a private commitment and will give an example of this, which will encourage their colleagues' motivation. Maybe motivation, comparable to what in other activities is created in our Stages of *Nourishing the Sense of God* and of *Motivation* may be generated, in addition, by emphasising in teaching the crucial significance of religion as a phenomenon in the contemporary world, as well as in history.

In our presentation of the Stage of *Learning* we introduced the idea of the ruling conception of a faith.[20] It is important that this conception remains fresh in the students' minds as they proceed into the depth and detail of specialised scholarship. Otherwise there is a danger of failing to see the wood for the trees and of confusing theology or Religious Studies with a desiccated concentration on ancient texts, languages and history! If the *Academic Study of Religion* is to contribute to a liberal education at the undergraduate level, the several dimensions of the ruling conception of one religion, let alone of other faiths, should not be lost sight of.

Finally it goes without saying that in Higher Education, as in *Religious Education*, *Learning* should not advance far unless it leads to *Exploration*. Naturally now in this context this *Exploration* will be at a sophisticated level. Religious truth-criteria, whatever they are thought to be, must be presented systematically, explained and their philosophical foundations fully investigated. If our Theory has any cogency in its application to Higher Education, philosophy of religion, doctrine and systematics must have a central place in Religious Studies and theology, so as to ensure that the most important issues are focused on and explored in a really profound way.

(vii) Ministerial Formation

Ministerial Formation is training for the ordained, professional Ministry of the church or for other kinds of full- or part-time paid or voluntary work in the institutional church. Such training usually has to be at the level of Higher Education and to provide a firm professional Christian identity for the potential Minister.[21] The aim is not only to equip future clergy and other workers with the professional skills they will need but also with a habitus,[22] a capacity to think theologically about Christian belief and practice and a propensity to go on reflecting on their faith and practice:[23] both their pastoral skills and devotion can then be shaped autonomously as they go on theologising throughout their careers.

This objective requires the radical revision of theological and pastoral training as it is.[24] Students and other critics claim that there is need to get away from a theology, which is presented as a set of disconnected academic disciplines, unrelated to life and practice. When candidates for Ministry finally give up their studies, it is said that they close their textbooks, pass their last examinations and cease to think critically about their faith on leaving college. Students should, it is suggested, move away from the traditional four-fold scheme of Biblical Studies, Doctrine, Church History and Pastoral Theology into a more integrated form of theologising. Their pastoral skills should also derive from the pastor's theological thinking: they should not just be modelled uncritically on others' example, 'sitting by Nelly'. And certainly pastoral practice ought not to be merely the product of thinking in the social sciences![25] Ministerial dealing with people must emerge rather from reflection on the Minister's faith.

There is also an apparent paradox in our conception of *Ministerial Formation* as a species of religious communication. On the one hand *Ministerial Formation* is a form of advanced *Nurture* and as such presupposes commitment. On the other hand this species of communication also belongs to the *Academic Study of Religion*, which does not assume any kind of faith or commitment. As was pointed out in our earlier discussion of the passage from *Exploration*, with its possible result in provisional belief, to *Commitment*,[26] there is no necessary contradiction here. In Higher Education, when the *Academic Study of Religion* is under way, although religious commitment cannot be presupposed, it cannot be excluded.

What is critical is that basic belief and ultimate commitment come under the severest scrutiny. First, however, the more elementary of our Stages of Communication have to be satisfied before the Communicatee is in a position to examine his or her own deepest faith. Selection for Ministry ensures sufficient *Verbal Ability*, a prior requirement for entering a form of Higher Education. *Autonomy*, another *Background Condition*, should be present to a high degree, either before training begins or being developed along with it. For Ministers are professionals, exercising rational judgement as they pursue their vocation, having to judge for themselves how to act as situations arise, without close control by tradition or authority. *Opportunity* to learn and to explore is provided by a period in Higher Education, either given by a residential place at college or university or offered at home as in non-residential forms of ministerial education in the UK or in Theological Education by Extension overseas.

A highly nourished Sense of God and adequate motivation can be assumed in anyone selected as having a vocation to Ministry (though, as in the *Academic Study of Religion*, tutors may have to help in sustaining motivation at times of stress and difficulty). As in *Nurture*, *Learning* begins with our ruling conception of religion. So far as is compatible with the demands of graduate study in Religious Studies and in Theology, *Ministerial Formation* needs a deepened all-round knowledge of the potential Minister's religion rather than academic specialisation – although motivation and deeper understanding of a faith can sometimes be promoted when students are allowed to follow their heads and go down a narrow road that fascinates and intrigues them! Yet a comprehensive competence in theology is usually the best equipment for the career of a general practitioner and is the best foundation for the profound exploration that is also needed. Obviously this knowledge is to be acquired as Higher Education proceeds, whether in the form of Religious Studies or Theology, and is the context for simultaneous or subsequent *Exploration*.

Ministerial Formation should begin this *Exploratory* phase with Religious Studies which would be put under our communicative category of the *Academic Study of Religion* in university or college. In such studies the Communicator and Communicatee are not necessarily believers in any faith. This type of Higher Education is just an open forum and market-place of ideas, in which faith is rigorously criticised (as, of course, it can be also in theology courses).[27] Here the candidate for Ministry can have his or her own beliefs powerfully nurtured or undermined. The candidate receives from Religious Studies a panoramic picture of faiths, and phenomenological, sociological and philosophical analysis of religion in the modern world. Many deep and searching questions about his or her own faith are bound to result. Under these stresses – with whatever pastoral support and guidance the candidate may need to prevent these strains from becoming overwhelming – his or her own spiritual identity can be hammered out ready for the challenges of future Ministry in a critical and open modern society.

This putting a candidate's faith at risk *can* happen in the course of *Exploration*, as we have already discussed in Section (**iii**) on *Nurture*. In *Ministerial Formation* this severe testing of faith should be a deliberate objective of the process. The greatest intellectual challenges the future Minister is likely to meet ought to be undergone in training, in so far as the future criticisms the believer may encounter can be anticipated in the present. Having once gone through the fires, the man or woman under training will have some experience of how to cope with similar questions and problems in future. Thus if the candidates emerge with their faith strengthened and their belief and integrity preserved, they are ready to move on to a more vocational and theological phase of training.

The Minister in training then needs an induction in theology in a theological college or its equivalent. Theology, in distinction from Religious Studies, does not 'bracket out' (or exclude consideration of) the truth of basic doctrine, but rather argues for or assumes positive belief, explores its ramifications and proceeds hand in hand with worship and personal counselling in supporting and completing the new Minister's professional formation.[28] Here if anywhere he or she should get helpful and constructive answers to the questions Religious Studies has raised in their minds.

Theology is the study of God and Christian theology an explication of what God is and has done in Christ. The process of argumentation begins from the Christian foundation-teaching as already described[29] and also draws on later reflection on that foundation-teaching. So the foundation-teaching plus this subsequent reflection down the ages together constitute the Christian tradition. The various departments or specialised disciplines of theology are all aspects of the study of this tradition. Bible Study has a central role and logical priority because it studies the ancient texts that crystallise the foundation-teaching; and material from this study flows into the other disciplines as they proceed to examine various facets of the developing tradition of the Christian community, such as Doctrine, Church History, Liturgy, Ethics, Spirituality and Mission etc. All these specialist disciplines carry out historical analysis (sometimes also literary, where texts are concerned) to identify the contents of tradition; to describe and formulate it; and to expound it against its social and cultural background.

When, however, theology itself, in the shape of all these disciplines, moves beyond historical analysis, the Kantian distinction between theory and practice is crucial. Theory derives from these historical sources and justifies what is to be believed: practice what is to be done. In theoretical theology, we argue from the Christian (or other) tradition to what we can reasonably believe today about God, using truth-criteria such as those suggested above.[30] Practical theology also draws on the historical special disciplines of Bible Study and the rest and gives reasons for action in the spheres of Ethics, Liturgy, Spirituality, Mission and Pastoral Work etc. Thus, for example, Liturgy discovers the history of forms of worship by the study of texts and their background. Theoretical theology then proceeds to ask what is worship, why should we worship: and practical theology elaborates how to construct and conduct worship, so moving finally from history to practice via theory. Theology is then a tree: scriptural study is its roots; the historical special disciplines trunk and branches; theory or theoretical theology the foliage; practice or practical theology the blossom or fruit.

To assist candidates for Ministry to become self-sufficient in theologising for themselves, they need to be introduced to a reasonable balance between the historical disciplines one with another and also with the theoretical and practical aspects of theology.[31] It must further be noted that practical theology needs for its conclusions, in addition to the Christian tradition, empirical premises from the social sciences. In drawing on these resources in support of practical propositions in theology, our three pre-religious criteria become important.[32] Before the social sciences can be utilised, issues of consistency between e.g. the Christian account of humanity and Freudianism or Behaviourism need resolution: is prayer merely an expression of wishful thinking to a non-existent fantasy father-figure in the sky and the divine response just suggestion or self-hypnosis in disguise? Can grace and the guidance of the Holy Spirit be reduced to schedules of reinforcement and of operant-conditioning in the subject by a religious community and tradition?

Again certain values associated with the human sciences in connection with e.g. personal responsibility, crime and punishment, mental illness and child-development have to be assessed against the explorer's pre-existent moral convictions in the same way as values coming from the tradition have to be evaluated. In the student's mind there has to be a dialectic between these prior norms, those faith proposes and those social science assumes. Reflection has to seek for new values to hold with integrity, whether those already in a person's conscience, or ones fresh to him or her, by creatively modifying their former convictions in discussion.

The third pre-religious criterion of historicity needs applying and extending, so that when practical theology demands historical or social facts, as e.g. about marriage in modern conditions, proper standards of statistical and historiographical rigour can judge conclusions concerning Christian practice and policy.

While training a Minister, the findings of practical theology have to be applied in pastoral practice by students, so that they may develop professional judgement.[33] This is best acquired by working with an experienced practitioner on some kind of fieldwork, on the apprenticeship model, in learning how flexibly to apply knowledge to real and ever-changing situations.[34] Such a process will be neither unthinkingly traditional nor authoritarian, if student and mentor are working with a proper theological rationale of practice that *both* believe is true and well founded. Thus in college a hospital chaplain may lead a theological discussion on Christian healing and then show how it is actually enacted in hospital.

Another important distinction in theology, beyond that between theory and practice, is that within practical theology between applied theology and a dialectical or hermeneutic approach.[35] Applied theology starts from the tradition and proceeds, as is commonly said 'deductively', that is to expound belief about what ought to be done on ethical, educational and pastoral matters from this tradition on particular topics or to exhibit its systematic unity across all the concerns of faith. It is indeed hard to see how the student can begin to learn to think theologically or lay foundations of general competence for his or her own theologising, except on some such planned and comprehensive basis. But the potential Minister also needs to be familiar with the so-called 'inductive' approach of taking a concern or problem in the modern world; discussing it with the congregation and expert consultants; becoming aware of everyone's presuppositions; and then employing the Christian tradition to situate this concern, to illuminate it and to justify action about it. This approach is known as dialectical or hermeneutic theology and it often appeals more to the less academically minded student. It is also a precedent and pattern for much of the professional thinking he or she will be called to do in future. Yet it is important to notice that dialectical or hermeneutic theology can be just as rigorous and academically respectable as any work in applied theology.

A final distinction in theology that it is profitable to make in connection with *Ministerial Formation* is between the academic and informal approaches. To introduce students to standards of rigour and precision in thinking, they must become familiar with scholarship and its apparatus of books, lectures, essays, examinations etc. that comprise studies in Higher Education. Candidates for Ministry should always be able to invoke the academic approach, if they choose, when they want in future to explore for themselves.

However, in church life and in much of their own thinking during their future careers, their habitus or capacity for theological thought will have to be exercised in what we term informal theology. This is oral discussion of the kind that can be developed with people in the local church, who may not be academic or highly educated but who need assistance in thinking out their Christian discipleship. It may also be the case that the less academic student will always be happier to theologise in this informal mode, by discussion and through more popular and less demanding books, in nurturing his or her own faith and prayer.

Ministerial Formation should then take students, via Religious Studies where their own faith will be put to the test, through Theology with its historical, and then its theoretical and practical aspects, to learning how to apply the Christian tradition to new concerns or to bring them in touch with the tradition; and how to go on thinking theologically in both academic and informal mode in their future career. This whole process of Religious Study, followed by theology, would then count as *Nurture*, because it takes for granted the initial commitment to faith of this sort of student. This previous formation is forged into a Minister's professional identity by first putting it through the fires of Religious Studies in a secular university or college, and then by annealing or strengthening it by theological discussion in the seminary, non-residential course or Theology by Extension setting, thus providing an enduring lifelong basis for further *Exploration* and ever-deepening *Commitment*, whether or not the commitment reached is formalised by Ordination or some such public ritual.

****

We have now discussed the application of our Stage Theory to *Evangelism*, *Inter-Faith Dialogue*, *Nurture* of adults, *Child Nurture*, *Religious Education*, the *Academic Study of Religion* and *Ministerial Formation*. After considering objections to our Theory and how to train the Communicators, it is only necessary to draw out our main conclusions and to place them in a wider, Christian setting.

Notes

[1] v. **1** (iii).
[2] v. **5** (ll) and (18).
[3] Brooks, G., Gorman, T., Harman, J., Hutchinson, D., Wilkins, A. (1996), *Family Literacy Works*, Basic Skills Agency, London.
[4] v. **4** (ii) (a).
[5] v. **5** (i).
[6] Cracknell, K. (1986), *Towards a New Relationship*, Epworth Press, London, **6**; Hooker, R. and Lamb, C. (1986), *Love the Stranger*, S. P. C. K., London, 102–117; Ariarajah, W. (1985), *The Bible and People of Other Faiths*, W. C. C., Geneva, **4–7**; Camps, A. (1983), *Partners in Dialogue*, Orbis Books, Mary Knoll, New York, **Pts. I** and **II**.
[7] Cracknell, op. cit., **6**; Hooker and Lamb, op. cit., 102–104.
[8] D'Costa, G. (1986), *Theology and Religious Pluralism*, Blackwell, Oxford, 118–121.
[9] Cracknell, op. cit., 123–127; D'Costa, op. cit., 121–125.
[10] Ibid., 126, quoting from (1978), *The Open Secret*, S. P. C. K., London, 211.
[11] Abraham, op. cit., **5**.
[12] Astley, J., Francis, L. J., Burton, L. and Wilcox, C. (1997), Distinguishing between Aims and Methods in Religious Education: a Study among Secondary Religious Education Teachers, in the *British Journal of Religious Education*, **19. 3**, 171.
[13] v. **6** (iv) esp. (20).

[14] Circular 1/94, (1994), *Religious Education and Collective Worship,* Department for Education, London, §17; Education Reform Act 1988, s.2 (1) (a).

[15] Dearing, R. (1994), *The National Curriculum and its Assessment*, Schools Curriculum and Assessment Authority, London, 41, §5. 3.

[16] Francis, L. J. and Lewis, J. M. (1996), Who Wants Religious Education? A Sociopsychological Profile of Adolescent Support for Religious Education in Astley, J. and Francis, L. J. Eds., *Christian Theology and Religious Education,* S. P. C. K., London, 223–246.

[17] v. **4** (ii)

[18] v. **6** (vi). Cf. Hebblethwaite, op. cit., 3–6.

[19] Smart, N. (1981), *Beyond Ideology,* Collins, London, **1, 2, 9** and Postscript.

[20] v. **6** (i).

[21] Astley, Francis, Crowder Eds., op. cit., **8.2, 8.3, 9.1, 9.2, 9.3.**

[22] Farley, E. (1983), *Theologica: The Fragmentation and Unity of Theological Education,* Fortress Press, Philadelphia, 35–36, 55; Hough, J. C. and Cobb, J. B. (1985), *Christian Identity and Christian Education,* Scholars Press, California, 3–5; Kelsey, D. H. (1992), *To Understand God Truly: What's Theological about a Theological School,* Westminster/John Knox Press, Louisville Kentucky, 126, 185.

[23] Farley, op. mcjrgnfj cit., **1, 6**; Hough and Cobb, op. cit., **1**; Advisory Council for the Church's Ministry (1987), Occasional Paper No. 22, *Education for the Church's Ministry,* Church House, London, 37–40.

[24] Farley, op. cit., **7, 8**; Hough and Cobb, op. cit., *104–109;* Kelsey, op. cit., 125–126, 166–172; A. C. C. M. Paper No. 22, op. cit., 15–21, 35–37.

[25] Ballard, ed. P. H. (1986), *The Foundations of Pastoral Studies and Practical Theology,* Board of Pastoral Studies, University College, Cardiff, **Pt III**.

[26] v. **7** (v).

[27] Cf. Mackinnon, D. (1972), Theology as a Discipline of a Modern University, in Shanin, T. Ed., *The Rules of the Game,* Tavistock Publications, London, 164–175.

[28] Ibid. **10**. Cf. also Smart, N. (1973), *The Phenomenon of Religion,* Macmillan, London, **1**, where 'Religious Studies' is called 'Religion'; v. also Hebblethwaite, B., op. cit., 1–3.

[29] v. **7** (iii) b.

[30] v. **7** (iii).

[31] A. C. C. M. Paper No. 22, op. cit., 38–41, 43–44.

[32] **7** (iii a).

[33] Hough and Cobb, op. cit., 117–129; Ballard, op. cit., **Pts II, IV**; A.C.C.M. Paper No.22, op. cit.,34, 41–42.

[34] Luntley, M. (2000), *Performance, Pay and Professionals,* Philosophy of Education Society of Great Britain, London, **4, 5**; Schon, D.A. (1983), *The Reflective Practitioner,* Harper Collins, USA 1983, **2, 5, 7, 9, 10**.

[35] Groome, T. H.(1989), A Religious Education Response, in Browning, D. S., Polk, D., Evison, I.S Eds., *The Education of the Practical Theologian,* Scholars Press, Atlanta Georgia, 83–91; Ballard, op. cit., 43–51, 72–77, 132–139; Browning D., (1991), *A Fundamental Practical Theology,* Fortress Press, Minneapolis.

Chapter 9

Objections

In this Chapter we consider and try to answer four objections to our Theory of Religious Communication. (All arise in a context of Christian use of the Theory; those of other faiths may be able to find their own parallels.) The first two objections are theological. The first objection is that in discussing communication we ignore the Social Gospel. The second is that we give no scope to the grace of God and the gifts of the Spirit in the communicative enterprise. The last two objections are practical. The third is the local churches' (and other Communicators') lack of resources and means to carry into effect the diversity of tasks the different Stages of our Theory demand. And the fourth is that Communicators will often find that the Communicatees have not yet reached the later Stages and still have to be treated by those working at the later stages as if further advanced along the road than in fact they are: it is like trying to build the higher storeys when the foundations and lower floors in a building are incomplete.

(i) The Social Gospel

It is widely held today that the mission of the church has two aspects: *Evangelism* and social action.[1] Thus we may be accused in our discussion of *Evangelism* and *Nurture*, both of adults and of children, of failing to give any consideration of the social responsibility aspect of mission and so of appearing to present a one-sided impression of the churches' communication task.

This accusation is, however, misplaced because we have never given any account of the content to be communicated, beyond claiming that it is a message expressed in words. All that we now need to do, to answer the objection, is to point out that this message, this packet of Christian beliefs and values, can and must include the social dimension. The kerygma contains the Social Gospel which is part of the good news of the kingdom.[2] The ruling-conception of the Christian religion will not have been adequately passed on in *Evangelism* or elaborated in *Nurture* unless the Gospel's social claims form a key part of what is to be learnt. This is as true of *Inter-Faith Dialogue, Religious Education,* the *Academic Study of Religion* and *Ministerial Formation,* as it is of *Evangelism* and *Nurture:* for all these activities are equally concerned with Christianity in its contemporary manifestation and in the twentieth century the church has discovered social responsibility as part of the gospel.

It should also be noted that the establishing of the kingdom in a given time and place never requires religious communication of the type presenting the personal challenge of the gospel does. Committed Christians can work with others, who are not committed Christians, to improve the structures of society to approximate more to what kingdom values dictate. Some non-Christians can share in this enterprise, because they have similar social values to the church and agree with its concern for justice, peace, the environment and the eradication of poverty. Having these values and aims does not entail Christian belief or even knowledge of it. It is a fact of common observation that believers can work with people of goodwill for kingdom purposes over many years without any communication of the gospel occurring in its more personal aspect.

What has also to be appreciated, however, is that for the church to be able to seek the kingdom in every place and time requires in practice the availability of significant numbers of committed Christians with the ability, leisure and energy to undertake this part of the church's mission. And unless the communicative enterprises of *Evangelism, Child Nurture* and *Ministerial Formation* are effectively carried out, in the long run the supply of such Christian community-workers, activists and prophets will dry up. Hence, those whose Christian calling is to concentrate on the church's social responsibility, should see the necessity for *Evangelism* and *Nurture* to proceed along the lines claimed for them by our Theory, so that the social aspect of mission stands some serious prospect of success.

(ii) Grace and Human Effort

The second theological objection to our Theory is that, by putting so much emphasis on human analysis and study of what communication requires and then by expecting Christians to undertake the tasks as thus outlined, too much weight is put on human effort and not enough on trust in God. In *Evangelism* and *Nurture* and the other species of religious communication, as we conceive them, what place is left for grace? In our conception of teaching for *Learning, Exploration* and for *Commitment*, what room is there for the gifts of the Spirit? We may labour at communicative activities, but surely God gives the increase![3]

At this point we need to place our Theory into an explicit theological context. Our analysis has hitherto been conceptual, moral and empirical, drawing on psychology, philosophy and commonsense in deriving our Theory and elaborating its Stages. Now we have to see our work in the context of Christian belief. Communicating and theorising about it becomes a church activity, a form of Christian service, a way of following Christ on his mission, a contribution to edifying the church.

In particular we must distinguish between necessary and sufficient conditions of success in religious communication. The force of this distinction may be seen from a simple example. 'Necessary' conditions of a good crop are factors like good seed, good soil, favourable weather, factors without which a good crop cannot grow. But such conditions are not enough, are not 'sufficient'. 'Sufficient' conditions will include any other relevant factors e.g. human ploughing and sowing, such that if all are present (with the necessary), a good crop must appear.

Clearly our Theory, even if it was fully applied, could only at the most secure the necessary conditions of any achievement in *Evangelism* or *Nurture*. At every point a multitude of further factors will control the success of the communicative process. The personality and background of the Communicatee, the material resources available, the talent, skill, training and attitude of the Communicator, the particular social and psychological factors on this occasion, and a host of other intangibles will be relevant to success.

When *Evangelism* and *Nurture* and the rest are successful, then sufficient conditions of success will have been present – this is a tautology. Now among all these further factors that determine success, including the mystery of the Communicatee's free response, there is left plenty of scope for grace and the work of the Holy Spirit. God indeed gives the increase and also offers his prevenient grace to the Communicatees, his help to these being granted before they respond (in the case of *Evangelism* and *Child Nurture* and perhaps of *Inter-Faith Dialogue*).[4]

Moreover, the acts of producing our Theory, applying it and using it in practice can themselves be seen as acts of grace. The more Christians serve God, freely and spontaneously using their talents and energies in Christ's mission, the more the grace of God is believed to be active in them. This has been called the paradox of grace.[5] St. Paul puts the point clearly: '...continue to work out your salvation with fear and trembling, for it is God who works in you to will and to act according to his good purpose'.[6] Paul thus exhorts Christians to strive hard, just because God is working his own good purpose in them. Hence, in our case, not only the sufficient conditions but the necessary conditions for success are gifts of

God. All is from God, even if not explicitly theological in description. God creates us with talents for use and service, including the multifarious skills involved in communication, even the reflection on what we do that gives rise to a theory such as the one we have produced. And then the exercise of these abilities is another example of grace.

These considerations apply, not only to *Evangelism, Nurture, Inter-Faith Dialogue* and *Ministerial Formation,* on the part of committed Christians, but also to non-Christians (and to Christians in public professional roles in a secular society) who teach literacy and oracy, foster autonomy and give *Religious Education* lessons or lectures or tutorials in the *Academic Study of Religion.* We have already seen in the case of committed Christians in private, who act professionally in *Religious Education* in schools and who lecture in Higher Education, that they can pursue a Christian vocation, while accepting the restrictions on their witness which education and university demand today. Moreover it is well attested in the Bible[7] that God acts through those who do not know him, whether we call this action grace, the work of the Spirit or the energy of the Logos in all creation. Thus service in *Religious Education* or the *Academic Study of Religion* is not a matter of human effort alone.

Hence we may conclude that when religious communication is placed in a theological context, this human activity is surrounded and undergirded by the grace of God.

(iii) Lack of Resources

The third objection we now consider is the first of the two practical ones. When the enterprise of communication is broken down into our eight Stages (the Communicator's, the second Model) and when a wide range of different tasks for the Communicator becomes apparent, a local church may feel it lacks the resources to undertake such a complex activity. So what profit is there in setting out so theoretical an ideal? What can a local church do significantly to influence child-rearing and education in promoting *Verbal Ability* and *Autonomy*? Can a parish provide the extensive witness and worship needed, of a quality sufficient to *Nourish* the Communicatee's *Sense of God*? What congregation can offer the range of activities to suit all the Myers-Briggs' personality types, so that individuals gain non-religious association with the church, to provoke the cognitive dissonance required for *Motivation?* Which local church has a plentiful supply of friendly, sympathetic, informed and committed believers with time to spare for *Inter-Faith Dialogue*?

Our main response is that it is surely desirable to be clear about the nature of any task and to see just what kinds of resourcing it needs. If our analysis of what religious communication requires is correct, the church as a whole will be better placed to fulfil this part of mission when everyone knows what the job needs in order to be tackled seriously. Frequently Christian communication fails just because it is not realised what is required to succeed in this enterprise.

What we have called early and later preparation for evangelism proper and nurture proper is necessary before the latter activities stand much chance of fruition. Conceivably some churches may be able to make available the resources required. It may be more a question of finding and training people for tasks not previously envisaged, than of an absolute shortage of funds and workers.

We concede it may be difficult for the average local church to do much about the first two *Background Conditions* of *Verbal Ability* and *Autonomy*, though many congregations run pre-schools, parent and toddler groups and extensive children's work, while some can influence their own Voluntary schools and even Community (State) schools in the neighbourhood: and in all these milieus *Verbal Ability* and *Autonomy* may be fostered. But at the national, regional and district e.g. diocesan levels the church can put its not insignificant weight behind literacy programmes and those trends in modern education that promote *Autonomy*.

Part of the Social Gospel is a criticism of current tendencies for education to become narrowly utilitarian and vocational, with the possible consequence that pupils become less independent, less able to think and choose for themselves. Of course, it is possible, nonetheless, that enlightened forms of testing and assessment should reward such powers of mind as creativity and originality, which are more than ever needed today when workers require broad skills and flexibility to change the type of work done several times in one lifetime. Hopefully we are pushing at an open door: to encourage in people what is good for religious communication is also to promote what young people need in a fast-changing world!

Opportunity, our third *Background Condition*, is surely something the Communicator can cope with, once he or she realises the need to be flexible and accommodating to meet the needs of the Communicatee.

What we have termed later preparation for evangelism proper and nurture proper has two aspects: *Nourishing the Sense of God* and *Motivation* by involvement in non-religious church activities. Any church can over time provide for the former. A quality of worship to make God real to the occasional attender is largely in the hands of priest and people, ministers and congregations. Indeed the kind of witness that will *Nourish the Sense of God* is a new requirement of Christians in their daily life. For this need it should be possible for churches to train lay people to show; by what they are, that God is real to them. And if we are correct in connecting this sort of witness with spirituality, the current fashionable interest in worship, liturgy and prayer can be turned to advantage: and in every congregation's programme of *Nurture,* teaching how to witness in this special way can be included.

The other element in later preparation, promoting *Motivation,* by involving the Communicatee in a wide range of practical and theoretical, cultural, social, recreational and community (but not religious) activities to suit all tastes, can build on what many large suburban churches already do. It may be true that in some small inner-city, council housing estate and rural churches, there will be little manpower to spare for this task. But since the majority of people are Es and Ss,[8] even small congregations should be able to get outsiders working in maintenance of church buildings and other practical, manual jobs. Perhaps this difficulty of mounting a broad spread of inviting occupations for benevolent onlookers, friends and relatives of churchgoers, is an argument for associating congregations together into larger units to make *Evangelism* and *Nurture* more viable. It could be the lack of such attracting activities that accounts in part for small churches managing to survive year after year but not to grow. Yet even the tiniest of congregations have some friends, neighbours and relatives living around them, and friendship itself may sometimes offer the association with the church that will provoke cognitive dissonance and so *Motivation*.[9]

With regard to *Religious Education*, the *Academic Study of Religion* and *Ministerial Formation*, we have already seen how these types of communicative activity require the *Background Conditions* to have been satisfied, if Communicatees are to learn, explore and reach appropriate commitment. Since the enterprises of education and Higher Education are publicly funded, are able to employ trained teachers and academics, and can use specially designed buildings and equipment, satisfying our first three Stages of *Verbal Ability, Autonomy* and *Opportunity* simply needs proper planning to ensure that the pre-requisites for successful schooling and study are provided. Nor should *Nourishing* the pupil's or student's *Sense of God* or *Motivating* them constitute insuperable difficulties for teachers and lecturers. When Communicators know what the earlier Stages of our Theory demand, sooner or later, they should be able to do much to make sure that their work is not like the house founded on sand, but rather like that based on rock.[10]

(iv) Remediation

It is of course better to build on a firm foundation properly laid. But in practice builders sometimes have to work on the superstructure of an edifice lacking such strong foundations and then it is necessary to try to make good this weakness, at the same time as completing the upper storeys. So we approach our fourth objection, the second practical one, that churches, teachers and lecturers often have to work with Communicatees at a later Stage, when they have not properly passed through the earlier ones. How can the Communicator help Communicatees through *Learning*, *Exploration* and on to *Commitment*, when it becomes clear that they lack *Verbal Ability* or *Autonomy*, or have a poorly *Nourished Sense of God* and do not possess enough *Motivation* to proceed? Hence the need for 'remedial' communicative activity, which can accompany our later Stages, supplying what has not been achieved at the earlier ones.

Suppose the church Communicator is leading a house-group or conducting an enquirers' group or a Confirmation/Baptism/Church Membership Class and finds its members lacking in *Verbal Ability*. In that context and in the short run, he or she can do little to improve literacy. But the Communicator can still, in the course of enabling *Learning* and *Exploration*, develop oracy, a crucial part of *Verbal Ability*, through discussion and through helping the inarticulate to express their thoughts. Remedial oracy is indicated and is indeed unavoidable. Permission to put their own thinking into words, even if wildly irrelevant and chasing after unprofitable hares, loosens the tongue-tied and gives the verbally shy the skills they need and faith in themselves. Here in *Learning* and *Exploring* it is important not to burden the learner or explorer with unnecessary complexity or the technical vocabulary of theology, as long as their point is made with sufficient exactness for the purpose in hand.

Similarly, *Autonomy* can be fostered in the course of taking the Communicatee through the Stages of *Learning* and *Exploration*. Giving people a chance to express their point of view, however incoherent and ill-formulated; giving space to people to think for themselves, perhaps for the first time; offering opportunities to see things in a new way or from a different perspective: all foster *Autonomy*. Maybe the Communicator can tactfully raise questions about the tradition in which the Communicatees have been brought up or about what it is fashionable to think today, and then challenge them: "What do you think?" Such moves, oft repeated, may give enough *Autonomy* for the time being to prevent *Exploration* from being nugatory.

There is no need to discuss *Opportunity* under this heading of remediation, since ex hypothesi the chance to learn and to explore is present. But to continue and to develop *Learning* and *Exploring* in further sessions may challenge the wit and ingenuity of Communicator and Communicatee together!

Now if the Communicatee has enough motivation to attend and participate in a group or class discussion of religious issues, a by-product of this process may be to *Nourish* their *Sense of God* and to get them to realise why God is so important at this present juncture. By courtesy, welcome and gentle reassurance, the Communicator may witness to his or her own Sense of God and pass it on in the small group. And in such a setting Communicatees may be open to an invitation to join in further church-related activity, which will get them to face their own ignorance and unbelief in the context of their friends' shared faith and to feel the dissonance which will make them want to go further. So where those who are not yet committed, or who are already committed but need to know more, are willing seriously to enter upon *Learning* and *Exploration*, the case is not hopeless and remediation to compensate for earlier missed Stages should be possible.

In the case of *Child Nurture* the above considerations apply but with important differences. The *Nurture* of *Children* extends over the comparatively long period of childhood and adolescence. Here there are ample opportunities to work on *Verbal Ability* and to generate *Autonomy* at any point and to postpone temporarily some particular venture in *Learning* and *Exploration* while remediation is attempted. And provided the child stays in the church ambit there will be endless further chances to make up lost ground (though if, by adolescence, *Motivation* is not fostered, young people are likely to leave the church and be uninterested in what is on offer).

Moreover in *Religious Education*, as in any other humanities 'subject' in the Secondary phase, remedial reading (or oracy) can readily be undertaken in a school or engineered to assist *Learning*. Now while it may be the case that young people from some sub-cultures lack autonomy, it may be possible to develop it, on the understanding that it operates in the classroom only. In this setting, pupils can feel free and safe to think the unthinkable and to imagine what it would be like to change their faith or to exchange belief for unbelief or vice versa. 'Classroom autonomy', only expressed in class, is no substitute for the real thing, of course; but if even a shadow of independent thought is cultivated over several years in school, who knows what pupils may come to upon maturity?

We have discussed earlier how hard it may be to *Nourish a Sense of God* in the Community (State)school[11] and this condition may well be absent, thus making it hard to motivate by cognitive dissonance in *Religious Education*. As we have admitted, other kinds of motivation – natural curiosity, analogy with existing interests, the desire to get qualifications – may make some *Religious Education* feasible in the Secondary phase. Such work can include empathy with the adherents in various theistic faiths as they face life. Hence our pupils can come to see how important God is to some people and hence how vital some religious questions can be to those who *do* have a developed Sense of God. Pupils can then be interested in learning and exploring by imagining themselves to be such believers. Thus, we may promote, by analogy with 'classroom autonomy', a 'classroom' Sense of God sufficient for *Religious Education* to flourish. Who knows the effect such mental experiments will have on pupils as they remember and reflect on these lessons in later years?

In the course of *Inter-Faith Dialogue* it could happen that a Dialogist suddenly becomes aware of his or her own lack of understanding of their own faith. Presumably he or she will then have the strongest motivation to undertake fresh *Nurture* in their own religion. And this can occur, either concurrently with the prosecution of the Dialogue or during an interval while Dialogue can be held over. Indeed informal contact and friendship between those of different religions may well be a powerful incentive to learn and to explore more in their respective faiths, so that as well-informed religionists they will be able to begin to dialogue! Perhaps it is not too utopian to envisage a day when inter-faith schools of *Nurture* and the A*cademic Study of Religion* may be set up in spiritually mixed communities to prepare believers for Dialogue.

Finally remediation has already been discussed to some extent with regard to the *Academic Study of Religion*.[12] Some of the ideas we have just developed for *Religious Education* could also work in Higher Education. Students who are not really autonomous could try to think for themselves in the security of a college or university context, so as to explore effectively, even though they do not feel free to do so elsewhere. Students with little Sense of God might be open to persuasion to put themselves in the shoes of believers in God and then would be willing to explore their faith, its articulation and the grounds that might be offered for it. Perhaps students could 'bracket out' and put on one side their own heteronomy and lack of interest, when entering Higher Education, and thus could be motivated properly to enter the Stages of *Learning* and *Exploration* of the phenomenon of religion.

In the case of *Ministerial Formation* the problem of remediation is more likely to arise with candidates who lack sufficient *Verbal Ability* because of their want of earlier formal education and qualifications. If motivation to become a Minister is strong, it will often be possible to persuade them to undertake extra education in literacy before beginning *Ministerial Formation*. We do not consider the example of the non-graduate candidate in detail: if such a person is worth training because of outstanding personal qualities, other experiences and achievements, and is not able to become a graduate for good reason, perhaps a special form of *Ministerial Formation* could be devised for him or her, with the academic approach to study of religion and theology being replaced by a more informal approach.

So it seems that remediation needed at a late Stage does not constitute a fatal obstacle to the application of our Theory of Religious Communication. Finishing this discussion of four objections, two theological and two practical, completes the presentation of our ideas. It remains to consider how to train our Communicator and, by way of conclusion, to offer our vision of religious communication in terms of a new image of what it is to proclaim the gospel in a secular age, as we sum up our argument.

Notes

[1] Sider, R. (1993), *Evangelism and Social Action*, Hodder and Stoughton, London.
[2] Abrahams, op. cit.,32 ff.
[3] 1 Corinthians **3**:7.
[4] Yarnold, E. (1974), *The Second Gift,* St. Paul's Publications, Slough, 128.
[5] Baillie, D. (1948), *God Was In Christ,* Faber and Faber, London, **5** (ii).
[6] Philippians **2**: 12–13.
[7] Isaiah **10**: 5–19, **45**: 1–7.
[8] v. **6** (15).
[9] Clarke, op. cit.,148–149; Finney, op. cit., 36–37, 43–47. Cf. also the discussion of this point in **5** (ii).
[10] Matthew **7**: 24–27; Luke **6**: 46–49.
[11] v. **5** (ii) (b).
[12] v. **8** (vi).

Chapter 10

Training the Communicators

The purpose of this Chapter is to discuss how the Communicators in the Theory are to be trained. We first consider the different kinds of Communicator and how much in general can be said about their common needs. Then Sections follow on each of our seven species of Religious Communication and with each we analyse the more specific training required for each of the eight Stages in our Theory. We work out what the relevant type of Communicator needs to know, to understand and to value and what they must be able to do, the skills wanted. Our approach is broadbrush. Because these training needs are so various and specialised, we cannot go into much detail, nor specify the actual technical literature and courses available, which will vary so greatly from place to place and time to time. We leave to others what actual modalities of training will produce the desired attainments.

One thing, however, can be affirmed at the outset. All Communicators need a sincere, deep, informed and committed belief themselves in the religion they are trying to communicate and, therefore, an appropriate education to gain the knowledge concerned. They should also have a clear grasp of the nature of their task, of the issues, and of distinctions and stages like those in our Theory.

(i) Who are the Communicators?

Who then are those whom in terms of our Theory we call the Communicators? There are four kinds.

The first variety are the 'Professionals'. In *Religious Education* there are professionally trained teachers. In the *Academic Study of Religion* and in *Ministerial Formation* there are professional academics and in these Species the task is undertaken almost entirely by the professionals.

Second are the 'Ordinary Believers' in or followers of a faith. In many situations, such as the *Nurture of Children*, witness, and perhaps *Inter-Faith Dialogue*, the responsibility of Communication falls on every adherent and thus every Christian. (In this Chapter, as in previous ones, our examples will be entirely from Christian practice: followers of other faiths can work our their own illustrations.)

The third sort of Communicator is the 'Enabler'. Their job is to train the Ordinary Believer. To do so, they themselves need to be Communicators in one or other of our Species and/or Stages, in order to be a model for Ordinary Believers to imitate and to know from the inside, from experience, what the task involves which they are training others to do. Clearly thus to train others, Enablers need a high level of training themselves.

The fourth kind of Communicator we distinguish is the 'Specialist' in one or other of our Species, when the job is not one for professionals. Thus some believers (lay or clergy) are gifted at these tasks and may feel a special vocation to be 'Evangelists' or 'Nurturers' of adults and children or perhaps to be 'Dialogists' with followers of other faiths. The last-named vocation may well be for a few only, although any believers' witness may extend a small way into *Dialogue*. Despite the key role of Ordinary Believers, elements in *Evangelism* or both varieties of *Nurture* are best left to Specialists, while the rest, or different Stages, can perfectly well be undertaken by any believer. (So when we say in future Evangelist etc. we sometimes may refer to Specialists, but not always: any Christian can play a part.)

Different kinds of Communicator then require divergent types or levels of training. The professional teacher and academic is trained in places of Higher Education in various standard ways. The training of Ordinary Believers will be in the hands of Enablers. The Enabler will often be the Minister and so he or she has to be prepared for this task as part of the education of clergy or church workers, which itself comes into our *Ministerial Formation*. The Specialist's training will in the first instance be the work of an Enabler, but in some cases e.g. of youth workers and Sunday School teachers preparation needs to be at a higher level.

So now we can proceed to look in turn at the special training needs of our Seven Species of Religious Communicators.

(ii) Evangelism

Our first stage in Evangelism is to generate *Verbal Ability*. Now, of course, any good parent or teacher will be concerned to do this, whether or not they are religious, simply as caring figures in home or school. The central task in the rearing and education of young children is the developing of oracy and literacy and later of broad powers of language. However, the religious Communicator will also take an interest in this task and will attempt to ensure that everyone will grow up and live as adults with a competence in language. For this competence is a foundation of all Religious Communication, the first *Background Condition* of our Theory. Hence Communicators at this Stage I will promote, where they can, *Verbal Ability* in every church pre-school, parent/toddler group and Sunday School, and whatever training they get for running these organisations, needs to stress the importance of *Verbal Ability* and how to stimulate it.

Our Second Stage of *Autonomy* should be the objective of child-rearing in a liberal society and is one of the chief aims of liberal education.[1] Autonomy is also what Religious Communication wants, whatever the faith of parent or teacher. Further, as with *Verbal Ability*, the Communicator takes responsibility for developing autonomy in all those he or she can influence. In church life generally, as in adult education, autonomy can be promoted by a style of democratic governance in the religious community. Since security, self-confidence and self-esteem all help underpin autonomy, the Evangelist, or anyone sharing in this Species of Religious Communication, needs to know how to generate these qualities in people. Indeed he or she may be able indirectly to promote discussion of all kinds in any secular community activity, as in public meetings, clubs and leisure societies of every sort, which will assist the growth of *Autonomy,* in those in whom it was not encouraged in childhood.

Furthermore religious autonomy requires the removal of gender prejudice that biases males against serious religious choice or even exploration. Our Communicator may need special aid in tackling such indoctrination in small children or young people or even mature adults. Training in this area could make all the difference to successful *Evangelism*.

Religious Communication, according to our Theory, should encourage or enable *Opportunity* to learn and explore faith. The first requirement is awareness of this step in our progression, so as not to assume blithely that everyone has *Opportunity*. Communicators need to be conscious of the ages and phases of life at which people have leisure, of social class differences and lifestyle factors that affect freedom to join Alpha and other courses, and of the special chances at the great transitions in life when folk are open to change and new thoughts.

The church has a message to give and believes there is a spiritual need that persists down the centuries, but this message has to be presented in ever-changing forms to people when they are able in practice to hear it. A part a Minister may play in *Evangelism* is to try to present Alpha or Emmaus courses[2] and to organise them in a user-friendly mode in ways that people can get to. There are many other domiciliary kinds of *Evangelism* from the Gospel Down The Street[3] to videos, Internet Sites, TV, audio-tapes and books, all of which provide *Opportunity* for the house-bound or those who cannot attend public meetings at conventional hours. Training may assist the Communicator to know what is on offer, to see the need to overcome the practical and logistical obstacles and to make it easy for everyone to receive the message.

Once *Opportunity* is available, our Theory claims we must *Nourish the Sense of God*. The crucial importance of this fourth Stage in our Theory has to be brought to the attention of the Communicator, particularly the Enabler, so that the bias of secularisation can be countered. Clergy can liaise with Religious Education teachers and head teachers on the fundamental need to equip pupils with an adequate concept of God not only for the sake of Religious Education, but also for any understanding of theistic faith that children may want or need when they grow up. This will benefit any groups in the community which have a religious message and enhance young people's chances to be able to understand and appreciate it.

Enablers, who are Ministers, also provide religious services, welcome non-churchgoers to infant baptisms, dedications and other birth-rites, weddings and funerals, and so make it possible for Communicatees to encounter worship. Thus training clergy in liturgy and the presentation of attractive, inspiring and enjoyable worship is required as another way to *Nourish* people's *Sense of God*. Above all the task of the Enabler is to train believers in the special kind of witness they may give to the reality of God by the sort of life they live. Clergy can aid the spiritual growth of Christians so they become men and women of prayer. Indirectly, therefore, courses on how to pray, retreats and similar conferences, can all aid *Nourishing the Sense of God* in those believers whom they are in contact with.

The followers of all theistic faiths should, in principle, share and cooperate in such tasks in a secular age.

Sometimes, indeed, an enhanced *Sense of God,* a more adequate notion of the divine and its importance, may lead to atheism and agnosticism when the real challenge of belief in God emerges and hence a need for apologetics arises. Some Evangelists and Enablers will need training in the philosophy of religion and in how to present the case for the existence of God. Current work in Natural Theology and Reformed Epistemology is thus relevant to *Evangelism* and studies by Enablers and Specialists in these areas may pay off in this context.

Now Evangelists, whoever they are, have a responsibility to bring about *Motivation* in the Communicatee. They should, therefore, be made aware of the importance of this Stage in Communication and also of the centrality of the Myers-Briggs personality typology (or of some equivalent) in this Stage, which will enable them to adjust their approach to varying kinds of people. Whoever takes charge of this Stage in *Evangelism* needs to co-ordinate and provide a wide range of church activities and also to ensure that church members have time and energy to spare for befriending outsiders, so that the conditions for cognitive dissonance will come about. Such a role will fall very largely on the clergy who require to have this aspect of *Evangelism* stressed in their training.

Evangelism at the Stage of *Learning* involves teaching the faith, the ability to explain and answer questions about it. Hence Evangelists need both intellectual and experiential knowledge of the faith being communicated. They should be able to run Alpha courses and other such schemes. The techniques of adult education and of modern catechetics need to be acquired by the Communicators, who have to be clear about the ruling-conception of the faith, which it is their aim to impart.

When *Learning* gives way to *Exploration*, as it is bound to do at many points during a course, the Evangelist needs to be trained in the skill of applying truth-criteria and of knowing which ones are relevant on a given occasion. Since full understanding here demands some philosophical sophistication, this element in this Stage is very much a task for a Specialist or Enabler, as it is at the corresponding point in *Nurturing* peoples *Sense of God*.

Often Ordinary Believers, especially those acting as mentors or companions of those on courses should be able to discuss and respond to probable enquiries or questions that may be raised by the Communicatees, even if they are not fully conscious of the truth-criteria being used. But the one who trains these believers, the Enabler, needs a full and informed grasp of the theoretical underpinnings, on the basis of which this objective aspect of *Exploration* is conducted.

When it comes to urging *Commitment*, the Evangelist needs knowledge of the distinction in the Theory between positive commitment to a faith and the educational commitment to further enquiry. At the Stage VIII in our sequence, the traditional Evangelists come into their own in urging commitment but have to balance this emphasis by pastoral care of the Communicatees who now have to decide whether, in the current state of their believing, faith commitment is more appropriate than educational commitment. Everyone involved, as at every other Stage, needs a clear understanding of what they are doing, and training is imperative in the nature of commitment and honest discussion of the pastoral issues concerned is particularly important.

(iii) Inter-Faith Dialogue

Inter-Faith Dialogue assumes *Verbal Ability*. Perhaps it is worth noting that one reason why it is important that everyone in a modern society, of any religion or none, has literacy and oracy is for the sake of religious learning and exploration when different faiths meet.

As with *Evangelism, Autonomy* is critical for followers of every religion and should be encouraged at home and at school. With adults remedial action to promote autonomy may be needed. When Dialogue begins, if one Dialogist suspects the other lacks autonomy, a pastoral approach combined with friendship and respect is required, so that the other can be urged to develop independence of mind. For it is hard to see how Dialogue can proceed very far without autonomy on both sides. The training of all believers in a multi-faith society will perhaps make those of every faith more aware of this issue and better able to deal with it sensitively when it arises.

Those who lead and plan Inter-Faith work and who organise meetings, courses and two- or three-Faith Forums, should try to maximise *Opportunity* for *Inter-Faith Dialogue* in such contexts. Ministers and other Enablers require in this training to know how to set up *Inter-Faith Dialogue* and to make ready believers for it. Friendship and social meeting come first and are basic. The informative stage should proceed before friends launch out on the dangerous seas of individual and mutual faith to faith encounter. Time has to be allowed for these people to bond and to share in common concerns of local community service *before* exploring religious differences. Thus training is needed in determining the order and balance of time and emphasis given between the acknowledged stages in *Dialogue*. An honest and sympathetic theology of how to approach other Religions needs teaching to those who prepare ordinary followers of one faith to encounter others, when these Believers may want help in setting up occasions for *Dialogue*.

Inter-Faith Dialogue takes for granted a well-Nourished Sense of God. Dialogue cannot begin otherwise, or people will not care enough to want to explore real issues. A possible exception might be with non-theistic faiths. Here we are in danger of exceeding the bounds of our Study, which is concerned with the communication of theistic religion. In practice occasions could arise if a Buddhist were to join an Inter-Faith group. There might then be a need to teach what God means to the religious theist and some examination of what the divine involves could be indicated. Certainly training is needed in theistic apologetics for *Evangelism* with secular people and Dialogists may profitably unite and cooperate with each other as e.g. children of Abraham, in commending belief in a creator to secular people. Perhaps indeed dialogue between followers of several theistic religions together with unbelievers may constitute a new form of *Inter-Faith Dialogue* (or *Evangelism?*) and some joint preparation for this enterprise may be possible – an utopian ideal, but who knows?

Inter-Faith Dialogue (additionally to *Verbal Ability* and *Autonomy*) clearly assumes *Motivation*: it can hardly begin otherwise. However, one curious possibility that might emerge could be friendship between a committed believer in one faith with a lapsed or superficial, not highly committed follower, of another religion. Friendship, plus this difference in religious commitment, might generate cognitive dissonance and then another type of *Inter-Faith Dialogue* could come about which might, for the second Dialogist, initiate *Exploration* in depth of his or her own faith provoked by their friend, the follower of another outlook. In that case, as with normal *Inter-Faith Dialogue*, the second Dialogist might need suitable *Evangelism* or *Nurture* in their own religion. Thus those who encourage or enable Dialogue in their training require awareness of such a contingency.

It might seem that the Dialogist would need information in advance about the other (real or potential) Dialogist's faith and this would have to come by prior *Learning*. Such knowledge would prevent gross inaccuracies and misunderstandings that could obstruct the opening and continuation of real Dialogue. Yet part of the aim of Stage II of Dialogue is precisely to learn about the other's faith *from* him or her and to find out just what its living core and force are for a particular, committed believer. There is a worry here that fresh *Learning* might be prejudiced or obscured by too much standard text-book knowledge of a religion in its world form, as opposed to the way in which the other Dialogist actually practises it in his or her local faith-community.[4]

Training for *Exploration* in *Inter-Faith Dialogue* will take the form of emphasising what progress can be expected in *Dialogue* and the patience and circumspection needed, when embarking on sensitive areas of theological difference. As *Exploration* proceeds each Dialogist needs to be aware of their own truth-criteria and the possibly different criteria the other is applying: and both should also be familiar with concepts like foundation-teaching, tradition in religion and divergent attitudes to Scripture. Indeed the Dialogist needs some theological and philosophical background to help when *Dialogue* about diverse religious teaching shifts to deeper cleavages over presuppositions. As the enterprise advances, the believer encountering the other's faith will need someone, either an Enabler or perhaps an academic, to act as a theological consultant at many points along the way to deal with difficult questions.

In *Inter-Faith Dialogue, Commitment* cannot be expected. It is conceivable though that a Dialogist might want to change their faith allegiance and pastoral help would have to be given. In view of all the sensitive and potentially explosive issues that can arise here, Dialogists should at least be trained to know of this possibility in advance and where to seek assistance.

(iv) Nurture of Adults

It is to be hoped that *Verbal Ability* can be assumed in a committed believer who comes for *Nurture*. However, in some cases, remedial provision is needed and adult education approaches, particularly those in basic literacy, will be useful. Nurturers, whoever they are, whether Believers, Specialists, Enablers and/or Ministers, should be made aware of facilities that are available and be able to use them, or even be involved themselves in this work.

Nurture also requires *Autonomy*. Hopefully this too may be taken for granted. However, with adults remediation in this respect sometimes needs undertaking as part of *Nurture*. Whoever is nurturing another will, in the course of deepening the other's faith, incidentally be cultivating autonomy and will help him or her hold their beliefs more autonomously. This indeed is one objective of *Nurture*. As well as theology, techniques of adult education are called for to promote people's thinking for themselves and these should enter the Nurturer's training.

All believers need the *Opportunity* for *Nurture*. Enablers and Ministers should be able to organise classes to suit the different types of person involved. Careful assessment of a person's needs, the kinds and levels of courses and qualifications available, should be part of the Nurturer's training.

When Nurturers sense that *Nourishing the Sense of God* is called for in their task, the fourth procedure, of making people more conscious of their creatureliness, can be employed to gain a deeper awareness of God's importance. If the Communicatee wants to have his or her Sense of God intensified, the Nurturer should employ the approach recommended to give people a greater awareness of contingency, and Nurturers need training in this approach. The Enabler may also have to help the Believer, qua Nurturer, in the defence of theism and should have some knowledge of contemporary arguments for God's existence and of the philosophical issues involved.

The Enabler also needs to be ready to see the possibility of cognitive dissonance arising as *Nurture* proceeds. This possibility can be exploited for further *Learning* and *Exploration*. For the sad truth is that many followers of a faith are quite uninformed despite their adherence and badly need *Nurture* but will not subject themselves to it unless they are motivated. Clergy do need to be made aware of the necessity to motivate their congregations and of the Stage of *Motivation*.

Those who teach at the Stage of *Learning* must have expert knowledge of the Faith they present to others, so that they are able to select material from a wide and deep acquaintance with it, to convey the ruling-conception and special aspects. Since this *Learning* in actual *Nurture* avoids a purely historical approach to the disciplines of theology, issues of truth and what a living faith requires also emerge. And Nurturers need to be trained not to pursue academic knowledge for its own sake alone but constantly to take into consideration its wider implications for life.

Exploration in *Nurture* needs a similar treatment to what should be found in *Evangelism*. Employing truth-criteria means the Nurturer should have knowledge of the distinction between the theological, philosophical, historical, social and ethical dimensions of faith and how to treat them. In an adult education framework, where students very much set the agenda and choose what they want to discuss, with *Nurture* this approach must be balanced by the need to deepen knowledge of the ruling-conception. So those who nurture have to be trained to proceed by both new and old forms of teaching, being used together in a sensible combination.

The Nurturer needs to encourage new forms of service and commitment at Stage VIII, our Stage of *Commitment*. The possibilities of Ordination and Lay Ministry should be held before the Communicatee. Students should be guided to affirm or reaffirm their positive faith commitment and at the same time to remain educationally committed to the search. In addition to training in Adult Education, the Nurturer requires awareness of these issues as they arise in our Theory.

(v) Child Nurture

Those in church who nurture children must obviously be alert to the importance of developing Verbal Ability in young children and of fostering Autonomy as they grow older. Work with the young in every kind of church organisation, as in schools and youth clubs, should aim at these abilities and propensities. Indeed the key point our Theory suggests is that the establishment of these first two Background Conditions is a large part of the objectives of the *Nurture of Children*, as well as socialisation into the religious community, the learning of facts, skills, the language of faith and the beginning of *Exploration*.

The Child Nurturer is ever on the lookout to provide new *Opportunity* to learn and explore. As well as training in Sunday School and Church youth work, proficiency is needed in the work of weekday groups, uniformed organisations, Christian Unions in schools and other para-church bodies. There has to be training to understand the pressures children are under in contemporary society, so as to find *Opportunity* for *Learning* and *Exploration* for those under the constraints that modern home life and the life-styles of the young can sometimes generate.

The upbringing of children in church should *Nourish their Sense of God* by worship and witness. It is also essential for the young to come to have an adequate understanding of the theistic way of interpreting experience and of the use of God-language. A Nurturer needs knowledge of these issues and a readiness to answer children's questions at earlier and later stages of childhood, plus awareness of how youngsters think at different ages.

As children grow up, *Motivation* is crucial, even with those in a religious community and from supportive homes. Natural interest, curiosity in what 'we' do with our parents and elders, will fade. In the light of our Theory cognitive dissonance between the developing young person's secular world and the beliefs of the church to which he or she is still attached will be generated, and *Motivation* to learn and explore will be energised. Not only Specialists in *Child-Nurture* but Ordinary Believers as parents, older friends, mentors and members of the congregation are of vital importance here. This witness to the churches' children needs to be helped by Enablers, who in turn know how crucial it is and who realise the significance of what they are doing.

When the young grow older, discrimination becomes important between the kinds and degrees of *Learning* to be attempted at various ages. Here the idea of 'levels of learning' can be an helpful notion. Something like the eight-level scale, recently produced for Religious Education in schools,[5] can be useful in suggesting levels of response generated in children in 'learning about' and 'from' religion[6]. With Learning about there is a marked progression from recognising the stories of a faith (Level 1) to being able to retell them in a child's own words (Level 2); from being able to abstract beliefs from stories (Level 3) to becoming aware of associated other elements in a religion and their expression in symbols

(Level 4); proceeding from knowledge of the differences belief makes to the way people live (Level 5) to consciousness of the diversity of belief within one faith-tradition (Level 6); from knowledge of a belief's historical and cultural background (Level 7) to finally being able to analyse and account for the influence of beliefs on people (Level 8).

For example, children first recognise the empty tomb as a Christian story. Second, they are able to retell it in their own words. Third, they know the story expresses the belief that Jesus rose from the dead. Fourth, they are aware the resurrection is celebrated at Easter and is symbolised by eggs. Fifth, they are conscious that belief in the resurrection gives hope and confidence in living. Sixth, they understand that resurrection belief is found in various forms within Christianity: interpretations run from a literal revival of Christ's body to merely subjective visions on the part of his disciples. Seventh, they know that Jews, who first preached the resurrection of Jesus, believed mainly in resurrection of the body rather than immortality of the soul. Eighth, they can analyse the impact of the resurrection on the church from the first generation to the contemporary influence of this idea. To be able to handle the material by way of these distinctions, training similar to that Religious Education teachers get is to be recommended.

A similar appreciation of different levels of thinking is valuable in helping children in the *Exploration* Stage. With Learning from they progress from identifying what they find important in a faith (Level 1) to appreciating others' responses to the faith (Level 2); from being able to compare their own reactions to it with others' (Level 3) to being able to raise their own questions concerning a religion and to suggest answers to these questions(Level 4); from making their own informed responses to these questions in the light of faith (Level 5) to reacting to inspirational religious figures (Level 6); from evaluating religious views on human identity and purpose in the light of evidence and examples(Level 7) to finally giving an informed and well-argued account of their own views (Level 8).

Thus first children discover that, like themselves, the disciples were sad at Jesus' death, as at any death. Second, they learn that Christians today do not fear death as annihilation. Third, they contrast their own and the disciples' grief at Christ's death with the confidence of Christians in the early church and nowadays before their own death. Fourth, the pupil enquires, "Did Jesus really rise? And how may this affect my attitude?"; and proposes his or her own answers to these questions. Fifth, children see that faith in the risen Christ could give them hope in the face of death and give informed reasons why Christians have this hope. Sixth, the explorer appreciates how e.g. Thomas was transformed by seeing and being able to touch the risen Lord.[7] Seventh, is the student's own preliminary assessment of the contention that a good God will not let his children see final destruction by death in conjunction with the NT evidence. Eighth, young people present a well-argued case from belief in God and the New Testament evidence to their own resurrection faith, in view of Christ's victory over the grave. Hence in *Child Nurture*, as children grow up, they explore when young, subjectively, what faith means to others and could mean to them; and when older, more objectively, the grounds for their faith and what underlies it.

Of course, unlike in *Religious Education,* the faith in which the child is being nurtured has to be central and other faiths come in by way of comparison and contrast: so children arrive at an ever-deepening understanding of belief and the ability to appraise it for truth, which is the chief aim of this Stage – though our subjective evaluation is also important, as in the lower levels of Learning from. Being capable of giving reasons for faith and taking account of the various tests there may be for religious truth are all matters with which the Child Nurturer should be familiar.

Sensitivity in allowing or encouraging *Commitment* is a key issue in training for *Child Nurture*. Children too easily fall into premature commitment. The provisionality of any commitment before adulthood is reached needs stressing. There has to be a balance between accepting the existential nature of belief in God and being able to pursue further the quest for truth. Caution about formal commitments, like Confirmation or parallel Church Membership rituals or professions of faith, is an important issue, which the Enabler of church workers and Ministers in their training should meet and grapple with. All involved should be reminded that this enterprise is not just *Nurture* but the *Nurture* of *children* into the possibility of *adult* faith.

(vi) Religious Education

Religious Education is normally conducted by professionally trained teachers. In this Section attention is drawn to aspects of our Theory which bear on their work and which, it is to be hoped, training (pre- and in-service) will take into account. To begin with the Background Conditions, *Verbal Ability* is cultivated by general education and is the responsibility of all teachers, especially in the Primary school. *Verbal Ability* is indeed essential for the success of *Religious Education*, as of all other subjects, and hence if pupils fail in this respect, remedial education is as essential here as elsewhere. This key point should be underlined in all teacher training.

Autonomy is equally important for success in general education and is a key aim of liberal education.[8] Peer-group pressures, social tradition, gender stereotypes of all kinds hinder the communication of religious truth, just as much as progress is blocked in the humanities, Personal and Social Education(PSE) and Citizenship by the lack of autonomy. Teachers over the years prepare for it and build up knowledge, skills and attitudes which are essential to it. In time pupils are encouraged to exercise autonomy in ever-widening circles on matters great and small. A special problem in all secular education is the lack of autonomy, which is encouraged and expected in some conservative religious cultures. Overcoming this difficulty is as important to *Religious Education* as it is to every other area where controversial issues are handled. Training teachers to help parents and the school's surrounding community to prize autonomy in the young is the best aid to Religious Communication in the sphere of *Religious Education*, as in other spheres, that can be given by the schools.

Law and government policy give pupils in schools in the United Kingdom (and in some other countries) *Opportunity* to learn about and to explore religion. The preparation of teachers, it goes without saying, should make heads, classroom teachers and subject specialists aware of the place of *Religious Education* in the Basic Curriculum, of the Agreed Syllabus machinery, the support of the Curriculum and Qualifications Authority (CQA), the value of public examinations and the danger of *Religious Education* being absorbed into PSE and Citizenship. If schools do what they are mandated to do, the *Opportunity* our Theory desiderates will be real: and professionals need to be made conscious of their responsibility as citizens to ensure that this serious chance for all pupils to learn of religion actually happens.

Gaining the concept of God is the concern both of the class teacher in the primary phase and of the *Religious Education* specialist in the secondary phase. The first crucial element in our Stage of *Nourishing the Sense of God* is to come to grasp this idea. Coping with pupils' real, philosophical questions about God as they grow up in a secular climate is a central part of *Religious Education* and a necessary precondition of Learning about and from religion. Worship and witness can provide incidental ways in the Community (State) school of *Nourishing* this *Sense of God.* This may or may not happen. When it does, the religious Communicator in church may be grateful for what school worship and *Religious Education* can offer of the first and second elements in generating a notion of God and of his importance, which is crucial for the communication of religion in a secular age – even if the pupil is led through *Religious Education* to doubt God's existence!

The key to the successful teaching of *Religious Education*, as of any other subject, is *Motivation*. Other motivations beyond that central to the Theory suggested here can be profitably used in school: the natural curiosity of younger pupils; association with students' existing interests; desires of adolescents for qualifications. Teachers, as we have seen,[9] are only too aware of how hard it is to motivate older, less academic pupils as their school-days approach their end. Perhaps there is scope for some sort of cognitive dissonance between young people's outlook and the spiritual dimension as they have discovered and come to appreciate it in the world's great religions. Possibly the training of *Religious Education* teachers should concentrate, not only on specific devices and gimmicks to open lessons to spark off an evanescent interest, but also on a long-term understanding of what faith can mean in pupils' imaginations and the gap between this and their own adolescent world view. In a secular age and in the ethos, especially of the Community (State) school, this gulf is difficult to overcome but at least its very existence, according to our argument, may assist in engendering a permanent interest in the religious quest.

Within *Religious Education*, our ruling conception of what is to be learnt is replaced by whatever conception of knowledge and understanding is given as the objective of the Agreed Syllabus for pupils to know when they reach GCSE level and complete their normal Secondary school course. As with *Child Nurture* the eight-level scale at its highest indicates what a mature comprehension of religion is like, when expressed in students' work. This standard is of an all-round concept of knowledge and understanding in several faiths and is the measure of successful *Learning*. The *Religious Education* teacher needs an awareness of such targets for his or her endeavours, parallel to those of the ruling conception which our Theory envisages for other species of Religious Communication.

Exploration is the heart of *Religious Education* and can be pursued at almost all levels and ages in school. Again the demands of the eight-level scheme have their exploratory aspect in that as the pupil proceeds up the series of levels the response has to be more and more thoughtful as the child matures. Our Theory distinguished a more personal and subjective assessment, equivalent to Learning from and building up a self-identity at the lower Levels when the pupil is younger, from a more objective interpretation of exploring religious truth at the higher Levels when older. This other target of Learning from is a reasoned personal stance on the 'big questions' and on moral issues. In preparing to lead and chair these discussions, the teacher could be worse prepared than to invoke some scheme of truth-criteria like those of our Theory and to be able, if called on, to defend them in the face of the searching questions pupils may ask.

If in the Stage of *Exploration* pupils come to beliefs like those of the great faiths, the possibility of commitment to one of them may be logically and ethically appropriate. The *Religious Education* teacher can then act as a counsellor on the steps a pupil, who is still a minor, may take to exercise his or her religious freedom in a liberal society, in view of peer and parental attitudes. Otherwise only the educational commitment to go on searching is suitable in school. Training must ensure in the teacher clarity on this point; and the proper place of thinking for oneself about faith, both inside and outside school, in the light of a pupil's religious background or lack of it.

(vii) The Academic Study of Religion

Academic staff are trained in scholarship and research and increasingly, nowadays, in lecturing and tutoring techniques, since assessment of teaching is now taken into account in evaluating a university department.[10] Do they need any further training in the light of our Theory, as it applies to Religious Studies and theology?

Verbal Ability is assumed at a high level in students. Scholarly skills are important, as is sufficient ability to construct essays and theses, but there should be an awareness on the part of staff that ability to think, argue and investigate ideas are still more central to the wider tasks of a university education. And it is these last capacities which are the form Verbal Ability takes in the context of Higher Education and which academics should be trained to recognise and foster.

Autonomy is taken for granted and will be encouraged in seminar and tutorial. Developing one's own ideas and criticism of material are basic to learning in the *Study of Religion*. There may be a problem indeed with students whose own religious position and background inhibit free investigation. Academic staff should be expert in giving help to students in thinking as mature adults in this kind of discussion and in knowing how to bracket out personal commitment when in the classroom; and training in the form of staff debates on their own teaching professionalism may be useful from time to time.

Normally academics do not have to take responsibility for the possibility of *Opportunity* for their own students. But today in Britain there are serious problems of student finance and debt piled up by young people at college. There are also fears of the relevance of religion's place in a university climate of vocational utilitarianism concerns. The claim of the overall Theory advocated here is that this underlying dimension of Religious Communication should not be ignored. Academics and graduates need awareness of their responsibility for Higher Education, in their role as citizens in a democracy, and as alumni who can assist the next generation from the fruits of their own past studies. Such considerations should not be beneath the dignity of the Communicators of religion in Higher Education!

In a secular age it is a real possibility that students have only an academic interest in religion and no wider sympathy. It is not inconceivable that such students may only wish to study religion historically or sociologically and may not desire to raise questions of the truth of the faiths they analyse and the claims religions make in the world today. Obviously from the point of view of the Theory this is inadequate. Whether such a restriction of concern for truth and a confinement to pure historical scholarship are also educationally sufficient is the crucial question. Unless the truth-claims of religion are taken seriously, it is doubtful whether either Religious Studies or theology can properly claim to be a distinctive discipline or afford one aspect of a liberal education at university level. And it may be questioned whether a student really lacking such religious interest in faiths as worldviews will have a concept of God adequate to make possible a full understanding in a course of academic enquiry. Thus it may behove tutors and lecturers to arouse someone's Sense of God, even without any theistic belief, in order to yield empathy for where believers stand. And as with *Opportunity, Nourishing* the students' *Sense of God* should be a matter of academic concern and fall within the subjects for staff training.

In the *Academic Study of Religion*, student motivation is taken for granted. Now if this fails, should undergraduates be left to sink or swim? If a university department carries any responsibility to aid students maintain their interest, then our Stage of *Motivation* becomes relevant. Perhaps with some students there needs to be growth from a purely theoretical curiosity about religion to something more existential in their sympathies, though not of course to actual faith. Conceivably there could be cognitive dissonance between such a limited interest in a faith and the appreciation gained from apprehension of what a great religion has meant to millions of humble believers. In the end an educational commitment to theological exploration may require such *Motivation* and staff might need training to try to help engender it.

What sort of *Learning* should an undergraduate pursue in the *Academic Study of Religion*? Is the aim of a university only to train students in scholarship, so that the few may become scholars themselves?

Some students may hope to become teachers, clergy, or simply to want a broad liberal education in theology or Religious Studies. In that case some general overview of the subject-matter of theology as a discipline and/or of one or more of the great faiths in several aspects is needed. This corresponds at university level to our ruling-conception of a religion and is required both as an introduction to and possibly as a summing up of the *Academic Study of Religion*. Here is matter for the academics' agenda in planning courses.

As with *Religious Education*, the *Exploration* of religious truth is the centre of theology, and in Religious Studies cannot be avoided if the sociological, psychological and philosophical perspectives on faith are pursued without restriction. Truth-criteria of some kind must be used, such as those presented above or some better formulation of them. Defence and explication of all our truth-criteria as an whole may not be fundamental to the purely historical or descriptive disciplines of the *Academic Study of Religion* (although e.g. the famous religious and historical criteria of Troeltsch,[11] applying the Enlightenment perspective on history to biblical material, are controversial today in New Testament studies).[12] Hence staff require consciousness of these factors in introducing students to issues of truth and may need training themselves – which should be internal to the *Academic Study of Religion* anyhow.

The Stage of Commitment applies to the *Academic Study of Religion*, as it does to *Religious Education*. The educational commitment to the pursuit of truth is the only type of commitment sought as the final end of this Species of Religious Communication. No positive commitment to a particular faith is sought or presupposed but may in fact be found. In the course of *Exploration* students' beliefs may change and any faith commitment of a specific kind may need adjusting. Since this process can be personally disturbing, not only in the transition from belief to unbelief or vice versa, but also in the move from a simple, unsophisticated variety of religion to a more rationally defensible kind, the welfare of the student should be a concern of tutors – if only to keep up numbers in the department – and some training in counselling is desirable. So even in the case of well-developed and autonomous disciplines like Religious Studies or theology, our Stage model illuminates certain problems students may have beneath the surface, and therefore, as well as their professional expertise, caring staff require training to cope with these matters.

(viii) Ministerial Formation

Those who train Ministers and undertake what we term *Ministerial Formation* will be academics and already qualified, like those who teach in the *Academic Study of Religion*. Naturally those who lecture and tutor in theology in the setting of a faith-community (whether in Theological College, non-residential Course or Theological Education by Extension) will be committed believers in the religion they are qualified to teach. It is also desirable that these Communicators should have reflected on the nature of their task and have embraced the kind of analysis found in our Theory or some equivalent account arising from their own thinking. Once again we now review our Stages to see what can be learnt from each and what extra preparation for their work tutors and lecturers need.

Verbal Ability is assumed, as the candidate for *Ministerial Formation* we take for granted will be an undergraduate or graduate. Should there appear promising potential Ministers who do not have the relevant academic qualifications to begin the course and so may not possess the appropriate type of Verbal Ability for this Species of Communication, pre-theological programmes of general education are required: or a less academic kind of training may be considered and experiments with a direct induction into informal theology may be attempted. This may well entail special preparation for academically trained staff!

Autonomy is crucial in *Ministerial Formation*, if the candidates are to learn to think for themselves as a professional and permanent requirement of their vocation. Furthermore, if their own faith during their education is to be put at risk by subjecting it to the kind of severe scrutiny a course of Religious Studies provides, autonomy is at a premium. For those not yet accustomed to exercise such independence of thought and choice or who come from religious traditions where the application of critical rationality to one's own faith is not popular or approved, this demand for intense reflection may be novel and stressful. Tutors can offer pastoral help and may need training in pastoral counselling of the kind that embraces not only psychotherapy but also spiritual wisdom in discerning how to criticise one's beliefs as a way of nurturing the creed one holds.

Opportunity for *Ministerial Formation* is arranged when the candidate begins their course. Problems of continuing funding, residence and family ties may occur during training. Clearly there is scope for the Enabler, whether the Principal or not, to take responsibility for guiding the student's practical progress and in our analysis this is part of his or her task as a Religious Communicator.

Certainly students need to have their *Sense of God Nourished* during *Ministerial Formation*, not only to improve their motivation but to deepen their spiritual lives, so that whatever their theology leads to in thought and conduct can be permanently energised. If candidates are to become Communicators themselves and to *Nourish* others' *Sense of God*, these students will require training in worship and also witness and spirituality, as they become the kind of person who is transparent to God. Therefore those who train such students in these abilities, who provide worship and a climate where God seems real, need themselves to be conscious of what the students want. As in Higher Education generally, the key form of staff training here is mutual help and debate among Communicators of Religion in the context of *Ministerial Formation*.

Those entering on *Ministerial Formation* should already be highly motivated. But their desire may be just to complete the course and to pursue their career, which they see in largely practical terms of working with people, administration and running local churches. Part of the task of *Ministerial Formation* is to generate a permanent interest in theology underpinning every side of their future professional work and to constitute a habitus, a capacity plus tendency, to go on and on thinking. One aspect or result of *Ministerial Formation*, corresponding to our Stage of *Motivation*, is to engender cognitive dissonances between the Ministers' own informed faith and their practice, as they become reflective practitioners.[13] For to perceive a gap between their daily activity and what faith demands need not be a source of guilt, frustration and failure but a stimulus, galvanising further thinking, as integrated professionals, on what they are called to be and do. This is Motivation to secure a living, life-long faith in the Minister and is what *Ministerial Formation* aims to attain. Tutors aware of this need require help to achieve this faith in themselves, so that they can help students find it.

A Minister should be a learned man or woman and *Learning* is a principal pursuit of the student during *Ministerial Formation*. The ruling-conception of the Ordinary Believer needs deepening and extending in every direction. Specialisation, if it generates interest and enthusiasm, is welcome but the final result should still be a balanced and comprehensive understanding of the Minister's religion. For the future cleric or church worker will be a general practitioner and resource-person in every theological field for his or her people. As before, the training academics on the staff need here is by mutual discussion and checking up on the Course programme to ensure that this requirement of breadth of study is met - which may not come easily to those who in the past have specialised in only one or two of the historical disciplines of theology. In *Ministerial*

Formation academic teachers have to ensure that every candidate is inducted into both theoretical and practical theology over a wide range of topics.

The transition within *Ministerial Formation* from Religious Studies in a secular and critical atmosphere to theology in a more supportive community of faith has already been sketched. Both phases of the critical stripping down of personal belief and the positive building of it up require more than academic help, if the candidate's voyage of *Exploration* and self-discovery is not to be sometimes traumatic, even endangering mental health and a student's new professional identity. The pastoral support of a personal tutor is essential and every staff member needs assistance in carrying out this vital role, especially remembering that students do not always approach for aid those officially assigned to care for them.

The end of *Ministerial Formation* is to help the student become a committed professional, possibly undertaking formal extra commitment by Ordination or by some other comparable ritual, while still retaining integrity, an enquiring mind and a tendency to go on thinking. Indeed the Minister above all needs to embrace the educational commitment to continue exploring. To serve others, Ministers have to persist in looking for God with heart, mind and imagination. In the end the way their formation can most assist them is by the example of tutors and also of the Ministers they meet on placement. To be themselves models of critical enquiry, not only in college but amid the pressures of ministerial work, the professional Communicators need the training that only mutual exchange of reflection and dialogue among themselves can give.

The future thinking of Ministers will be more and more (though never entirely) in practical theology, and their judgement has to be developed on placement in readiness for their future work. The Communicators here may be college tutors, experienced Ministers and Ordinary Believers in local churches. They have to share in the students' thinking and assist them in learning how to apply theology in real situations. For this vital task all parties need the training mutual consultation alone can give, plus what students have learnt from their own corporate experience in the work of a religious community. In this way practical theology and judgement form an integral part of the Ministers' mental equipment, to the exercise of which they become finally committed as the culmination of their *Ministerial Formation* in the Stage of *Commitment*.

* * * * * * *

Thus every Religious Communicator (except non-religious parents and teachers vis-à-vis *Verbal Ability* and *Autonomy*) needs special training of various sorts to assist in the effective undertaking of their task, at each of the eight Stages, in our seven Species of Religious Communication. This is in addition to a general knowledge of the faith they hope to communicate and to a grasp of our Theory or some better analysis of what they attempt. These multifarious kinds of training will be given in many different ways in many diverse institutions.

Indeed perhaps there is a case we suggest, by way of conclusion of this long discussion, for some central Institution in a Religion to oversee and coordinate training in Religious Communication, to carry out research, to disseminate good practice and to refine further the Theory we have attempted to construct. Such a body could bring to bear on the disorganised and spasmodic training existing churches give for *Evangelism, Nurture* and *Child Nurture*, some of the expertise and professionalism now devoted to the training of *Religious Education* teachers and even of academics employed in the *Academic Study of Religion* and *Ministerial Formation*. By careful attention to the resemblances and differences between our seven Species, new insights might be generated and fresh enthusiasms quickened. A central organisation could draw together the strengths of these various specialisms which at present are isolated from one another and immured in institutions that have no current mutual communication.

All that now remains in our Study is to summarise the general argument or this and earlier chapters, and to open up a final vision of this Communicative enterprise as it should proceed in this life and the next.

Notes

[1] Levinson, op. cit., **2. 4**.
[2] v. **6** (12).
[3] v. **6** (20).
[4] 8 (ii); Jackson, R. (1997), *Religious Education: An Interpretative Approach*, Hodder and Stoughton, London, **3, 5, 6.**
[5] Association of Religious Education Inspectors, Advisors and Consultants (1998), *Towards National Standards in Religious Education*, Bury; the Curriculum and Qualifications Authority (2000), *Religious Education: non–statutory guidance*, QCA/00/576 is the basis for the précis in our text.
[6] S. C. A. A. (1994), op. cit., Models 1, 2, Model Attainment Targets; cf. Attfield, D. G. (1996), Learning from Religion, *British Journal of Religious Education*, **18. 2**, 78–84, for a full discussion of this distinction, [though with conclusions the author no longer fully adheres to, as the main text of this book implies].
[7] John **20**: 28.
[8] v. (1).

[9] v. **8** (32).

[10] v. e.g. the *Teaching Quality Assessments* of the Quality Assurance Agency for Higher Education in the UK.

[11] v. discussion in Coakley, S. (1988), *Christ Without Absolutes,* Clarendon Press, Oxford, 24–27; and Harvey, V. A. (1967*), The Historian and the Believer,* S. C. M. Press, London, **I**.

[12] Harvey, op. cit.*, passim.*

[13] Schon, op. cit.

Chapter 11

A Concluding Vision

In this final chapter we first summarise the entire argument of our book. Then we recast it into a vision of religious communication based on an allegorical interpretation of Jesus' parable of the Sower. Finally we apply this vision speculatively to Christian existence in this life and the next. In this last phase of our discussion the argument is conducted on specifically Christian assumptions: we leave it to Communicators of other faiths to develop their own examples.

(i) Summary of the Whole Argument

Religious Communication is a genus containing seven species: *Evangelism, Inter-Faith Dialogue, Nurture, Child-Nurture, Religious Education,* the *Academic Study of Religion* and *Ministerial Formation.* In order to distinguish these communicative activities from one another, a definition of a committed, practising Christian was constructed step by step. We then set out the assumptions of this study about modern society and about the nature of the religious message.

Our Stage Theory was next derived and justified. It was presented in two forms: a first Model (the Communicatee's) of five Stages and three Background Conditions; and the second Model (the Communicator's) of eight Stages. These Stages are- *Verbal Ability, Autonomy, Opportunity, Nourishing the Sense of God, Motivation, Learning, Exploration* and *Commitment.* Each Stage in the second Model received separate consideration. We clarified the nature of each; we considered how in general terms it can be undertaken and when the Communicatee can be judged to have successfully completed it.

Verbal Ability was divided into literacy and oracy and the importance of child-rearing patterns and education was stressed. *Autonomy* was expounded in terms of being self-directed, as opposed to being tradition-directed, other-directed or inner-directed. The difficulties in modern conditions of finding *Opportunity* for communication were discussed. In a secular age *Motivation* to learn about and explore religion would not be secure unless the Communicatee's *Sense of God* was Nourished*:* and this might require an apologetic for theism. Then *Motivation* by cognitive dissonance would be possible, being generated in different kinds of people by a variety of suggested activities; and the Myers-Briggs' typology of personality was introduced to classify people appropriately.

The Stage of *Learning* was analysed in terms of a ruling conception of religion with four dimensions. *Exploration* was divided into personal assessment of a religion, interpreted as not necessarily making truth claims; and as assessment of the doctrines of faiths, when these are understood to be factual belief-systems, which do make truth-claims. We sketched truth-criteria for religion, both of a particular religion and between religions; the dependence of such criteria on a philosophical underpinning of religious truth was discussed; the situation clarified as to what would happen were that underpinning not to be available; and an alternative approach based on Reformed Epistemology set out. The appropriate types of *Commitment* for the various species of religious communication were explained, and we distinguished between a positive commitment to a faith and an educational commitment to the search for truth.

Our Theory was then applied to each of the seven Species of Religious Communication in turn and its practical application was outlined. Further programmatic distinctions were made between Evangelism proper and Nurture proper on the one hand and early and later preparation for these on the other. Special attention was paid to *Inter-Faith Dialogue* as a Species of Communication distinct from *Evangelism* and to the training of Ministers of religion as a development out of *Nurture* and as sharing with the **Academic Study of Religion** in Higher Education. In our discussion such training of Ministers has become a new Species of Communication in its own right, called *Ministerial Formation*. Finally, two theological and two practical objections to our Theory were considered and rebutted: and an extended account was given of the kinds of training, both general and specific, Communicators of various sorts need for the eight Stages in each of the seven Species of Religious Communication.

(ii) The Sower and the Seed

What has so far appeared as a rather abstract argument is unlikely to appeal to and challenge those who wish to communicate their faith. So now we present our Theory more in terms of a vision of what can be attempted. We take Jesus' parable of the Sower.[1] The Gospels contain what is usually regarded as an allegorical interpretation of this well-known story.[2] If the early church was thus able to develop and elaborate upon Christ's words, the church in later ages can surely do the same. Hence we will now try creatively to rework the parable for our purposes. We offer a presentation of the Sower as a first approximation to an adequate picture of religious communication.

In our understanding of the parable the seed is the message; God or the human Communicator is the Sower; and the diverse kinds of ground onto which the seed falls correspond to the Stages of our Theory in the second Model (the Communicator's). The unfruitful kinds of soil represent what happens if the earlier Stages are severally neglected. The core of religious communication, what we have called 'Evangelism proper' or 'Nurture_proper' or the taught content of *Religious Education* or of the *Academic Study of Religion* or what the Dialogist seeks to explain and *Ministerial Formation* to induct a student into, comprising our last three Stages, is the good ground that yields the harvest.

To pursue the analogy in detail. The path, when the seed lies on the surface and is eaten by birds corresponds to the Communicatee in whom the three Background Conditions are not satisfied. For, first, without *Verbal Ability*, the seed which is a verbal message will have nothing to grow into, no pre-existing mental framework in the Communicatee's mind to be received in. The seed will just lie loose and inert and be food for birds, like a totally uncomprehended message.

Secondly, again without *Autonomy*, the message may be understood but it will be ignored or rejected, because the culture in which the Communicatees have been brought up has not been challenged. Hence the word will be spurned because that is what everybody else in the Communicatee's peer-group does with it, or because the tradition they come from has no use for this message, or because the Communicatees cannot freely explore it on account of the prejudices into which they have been nurtured in childhood. This soil lacks the ability to receive the seed and to consider the word properly.

There is thirdly lack of *Opportunity* when Communicatees lack the time, leisure and energy to grasp the gospel-message, either because they can never hear it properly or because other pressures prevent them giving it due attention. The seed has no chance to be received into the mind and worked at with fresh energy and care. So the seed just lies on the surface, never penetrating the soil, and is soon forgotten, as when swallowed by birds.

What now of the seed that sprouts up well and then quickly withers because it lacks depth of earth? This is clearly Communicatees whose

Sense of God has not been *Nourished*. Attempts to motivate them fail because the theistic dimension in life means little or nothing to the modern secularised person. Perhaps they are connected with the church by natural curiosity or by working alongside a committed Christian in some good cause, and a spark of interest in religious matters has been generated. But it soon dies out, long before *Learning* or *Exploration* can proceed. The seed cannot put down strong roots for it lacks good soil, a mind in the Communicatees prepared to receive the religious message, to learn about it and to investigate it, since they think issues to do with God are not important enough to bother about.

Next suppose the seed does have depth of soil, that is a well *nourished Sense of God*. Will the plant grow healthily, with a strong and sustained interest enough to underpin *Learning* and *Exploration* that can produce ultimately *Commitment*? The answer is the corn will not flourish if the young shoot is choked by thorns and weeds, the distractions and preoccupations of modern living. An additional resistance needs to be injected into the soil so the plant can grow strongly and keep on growing despite the weeds. This resistance in the ground is the pressure of cognitive dissonance making the Communicatee want to learn and explore.

Cognitive dissonance can be generated in as many ways as there are types of person and temperament, as we have seen when we employed the Myers-Briggs typology. The key point is that, however it is done, a person needs to build up an association with the Christian community, which appeals to him or her as they actually currently are, having little religious knowledge and belief, despite their newly *Nurtured Sense of God*. Then their felt embarrassment, (the form that cognitive dissonance takes in consciousness), at the gap that they feel between Christianity, which they now think important because their *Sense of God* has been *Nourished*, and their own distance from the faith, turns into a powerful desire to reduce any paradox or discrepancy. Without such *Motivation,* engendered by depth of soil (a *Nurtured Sense of God*) and the resistant quality of this ground (the cognitive dissonance reverberating in Communicatees), the tender shoots will be overshadowed, choked and ousted by the thorns and thistles of non-religious concerns, the pressing exigencies of daily life in the twenty-first century in the west.

What happens when the seed falls into good soil, containing deep interest from a *Nourished Sense of God* and from the energy-generating power of cognitive dissonance? The parable claims some seeds multiply thirty, some sixty and some an hundred fold. We may compare this happy result with the outcome of *Evangelism* and of *Nurture*, of *Inter-Faith Dialogue* or of *Child Nurture*, or with the intended and possible result of

Religious Education, the *Academic Study of Religion* or *Ministerial Formation.*

Some Communicatees who have received the seed pass successfully through the Stage of *Learning* but do not proceed to *Exploration.* This outcome may be compared with the thirty-fold increase, a passable harvest but not the best, in whatever Species of Religious Communication we have in mind. Other seeds correspond to those who complete the Stage of *Exploration* but who either end up as informed and understanding unbelievers or as followers of Other Faiths, those tentatively believing but not yet ready to commit themselves for faith or against it. This is the sixty fold increase. Such a result is welcome in *Evangelism, Inter-faith Dialogue, Nurture* and in *Child Nurture*, though obviously not the very best that can be hoped for or intended in these Species (except in *Inter-faith Dialogue* where Commitment is not the intention.) And there is always the chance that Communicatees will take the last step later and commit themselves, or will explore again and then reach a definite positive or negative position. With *Religious Education, Inter-Faith Dialogue* and the *Academic Study of Religion,* the sixty-fold harvest of informed exploration is success indeed and is what is intended and hoped for.

Finally there is the seed which multiplies itself a hundred times in the harvest. This represents the Communicatee who learns and explores and who then reaches a positive religious commitment. This is the greatest success intended and hoped for in *Evangelism, Nurture, Child Nurture* and *Ministerial Formation.* It may also happen incidentally and unintentionally in *Religious Education, Inter-Faith Dialogue* or in the *Academic Study of Religion.* It is not the best product from the point of view and expectation of these three disciplines, but is consistent with a good outcome on the part of the pupil, the Dialogist or student who is informed and has significantly explored the issues.

At this point we may ask what is the point of our allegorising this ancient parable of Christ and of expressing our Stage Theory in terms of this story? Mainly the conclusion of our discussion is that the Communicator cannot in fact be adequately conceived of as a Sower alone. In terms of our Theory, teaching in the Stage of *Learning*, enabling or encouraging in the Stage of *Exploration*, and preaching or urging in that of *Commitment* can be considered aspects of sowing and the Religious Communicator has to do these things. Where the image fails, however, is in respect of preparing the ground. In Palestine of old the sower sowed broadcast before ploughing.[3] By chance some seed fell on good ground, whereas most landed on infertile or unproductive soil. Unless, that is, the Background Conditions are satisfied, the seed falls on the hardened path effect. If the soil of the Communicatee's mind is not deepened by *Nourishing* their *Sense of God*, the seed may grow a little but growth will not last. Should resistance in the soil not be generated by provoking cognitive dissonance, the young shoot will not endure healthily in competition with weeds and thorns, the counter-pressures of modern life, for long enough to come to harvest. The sower's efforts will be in vain.

A better and more comprehensive image than that of the ancient sower is to think of Communicators as contemporary farmers who deep plough and harrow, enrich and fertilise the soil, and who make it resistant before they sow. Our suggestion is that farming is a preferable picture of what it is to communicate religion to that of the sower, whether he or she be evangelist, nurturer, child-nurturer, Dialogist, preacher or teacher, academic or theological educator. Like the farmer, the Communicator must prepare before he or she sows.

(iii) A Final View

In this book Communication has been seen as a key part of Christian existence. In our analysis of what should ideally happen, those who become committed Christians do so through Religious Communication, either in the form of *Evangelism* or *Child-Nurture*. It is also possible that some of these pass through our earlier Stages in the context of *Religious Education* or the *Academic Study of Religion* and that the process is then completed in the church-sponsored enterprises of *Evangelism* and *Child-Nurture*. Once people are committed believers, *Nurture* begins and can continue throughout life and may be developed into *Ministerial Formation* in suitable cases.

What happens after death? Assuming there is an after-life, it is interesting to speculate on what becomes of Religious Communication during this post-mortem existence. If we assume that in the next world the truth of the Christian gospel is not obvious and evident to all and that the human mind remains as it has been shaped in this world by contemporary culture, something akin to Religious Communication can be postulated to occur as we conceive it in our Stage Theory. For committed Christians the Stage of *Nurture* may well continue in that first period of the next life which may be thought of in terms of education, training, purification and preparation for a final stage of beatitude.[4]

It is further worth considering, on the same assumptions about human nature and the problematic nature of Christian truth, whether *Evangelism* in the after-life is a real possibility. On universalist premises,[5]

Evangelism in the after-life is a real possibility. On universalist premisses,[5] all men and women, or possibly just those who have served Christ in this world in the guise of 'the least of these my brethren',[6] will need to come to a conscious knowledge and commitment to the Christian faith beyond the grave. Devout followers of other religions, who may have been in Dialogue with Christians, but who have retained their own commitment; saintly unbelievers; and the vast mass of ordinary people, who never advanced far beyond their baptism and who remained in this mortal life nominal, aborted or lapsed Christians – all have to reach a real and living faith in Jesus. These folk too have a necessity to proceed through something like our Stages, with their Christian friends from this world perhaps acting as Evangelists and Communicators.

Of course the assumptions we have just made may be wrong. Perhaps, after the grave, Christian truth is transparently obvious to all.[7] In that case, communication as we conceive it in this book is redundant and those destined for salvation, whether all human beings or some only, as soon as they open their eyes in the next world, immediately know and accept the saving truth of the Gospel.

Possibly we may wonder whether the situation may be different for different groups after death. For some the truth of the gospel will be at once evident when they enter the next life. Perhaps those who die in infancy or childhood, those who have never heard the Christian message in this world, and those who have never passed through all our Stages on the way to Commitment, may need to be in a place where Christian truth is still problematic, so that their response can be free and not forced by the overwhelming weight of glory.[8] In that case something like *Evangelism* in some or all of its Stages would still be required.

Speculation about whether and how religious communication is needed in the life to come may seem pointless. But such reflections are not entirely idle curiosity. Apart from their intrinsic interest, they also bring out again the crucial assumptions underlying our Theory. Minds need preparation, people need Motivation and a chance to Learn and Explore before Commitment can properly come. These requirements are ineluctable, given what human beings are and the nature of the modern world. No doubt in other ages the religious situation was vastly different and this may be true of other parts of the world today and was true of our own society until quite recently.

However, in the modern, secular, pluralistic and individualistic age we live in, in this world, whatever may be the case beyond the grave, religious communication should be a central task of the church. To carry it out fruitfully, intelligently and effectively, we should recall the parable of receptiveness to the gospel. Our case is that today the contemporary Communicator is best conceived as like a farmer. As the twenty-first century opens, the good husbandman not only sows, but also first ploughs and harrows, fertilises and prepares the soil, in the hope of a great harvest.

Notes

[1] Matthew 13:1–9; Mark 4:13–20; Luke 8:4–8.

[2] Matthew 13:18–23; Mark 4:13–20; Luke 8:11–15. Cf. for example Dodd, C. H. (1935), *The Parables of the Kingdom*, Nisbet, London, 180–182; Jeremias, J. (1954), *The Parables of Jesus*, S. C. M., London, 61–63; Hooker, M. D. (1991),*The Gospel according to St Mark*, A. C. Black, London, 129–130.

[3] Jeremias, op. cit. 9.

[4] Hick, J. (1976), *Death & Eternal Life,* Collins, London, 455–458; Hebblethwaite, B. (1984), *The Christian Hope*, Marshall, Morgan & Scott, Basingstoke, 218–220.

[5] Hick, op. cit., **13**; Hebblethwaite, op. cit.,213–218.

[6] Matthew 25:40. Cf. Yarnold, op.cit.,173–174.

[7] Hick, J. (1966), *Faith and Knowledge*, Macmillan , 2nd edition, London, 187–199; Hebblethwaite, op. cit., 222.

[8] Ibid. **6** for Hick's idea of "epistemic distance". Cf. also Hick, op.cit.(1976) 250–259 for a profound discussion of the issues involved.

Bibliography

A. C. C. M. (1987), Occasional Paper No. 22, *Education for the Church's Ministry,* Church House, London.
Abbott and Gallagher, (1965), *The Documents of Vatican II*, G. Chapman, London.
Abraham, W. J. (1989), *The Logic of Evangelism*, Hodder and Stoughton, London.
A. C. C. M. (1987), Occasional Paper No. 22, *Education for the Church's Ministry,* Church House, London.
Argyle, M. and Beit-Hallahmi, B. (1975), *The Social Psychology of Religion,* Routledge and Kegan Paul, London.
Ariarajah, W. (1985), *The Bible and People of Other Faiths*, W. C. C., Geneva.
Association of Religious Education Inspectors, Advisors and Consultants (1998), *Towards National Standards in Religious Education,* Bury.
Astley J. (1994), *The Philosophy of Christian Religious Education,* Religious Education Press, Birmingham, Alabama.
Astley, J. (1994), The Place of understanding in Christian Education and Education about Christianity, **2. 4**, in Astley, J. and Francis, L. J., *Critical Perspectives in Christian Education,* Gracewing, Leominster.
Astley, J. (1996), The Role of Worship in Christian Learning, in Astley, J., Francis, L. J. and Crowder, C. Eds., *Theological Perspectives in Christian Formation,* Gracewing, Leominster.
Astley, J. (2000), Aims and Approaches in Christian Education, in Astley, J. Ed., *Learning in the Way,* Gracewing, Leominister.
Astley, J. and Francis, L. Eds. (1992), *Christian Perspectives on Faith Development*, Gracewing, Leominster.
Astley, J., Francis, L. J., Burton, L. and Wilcox, C. (1997), Distinguishing between Aims and Methods in Religious Education: a Study among Secondary Religious Education Teachers, *British Journal of Religious Education*,**19. 3**, 171.
Attfield, D. G. (1976), A Taxonomy of Religious Concepts, *Learning for Living*, Winter,**16. 2,** 68–75.
Attfield, D. G. (1982), Conceptual Research in Religious Education, in Hull, J. Ed., *New Directions in Religious Education*, Falmer Press, Lewes, 77–84.
Attfield, D. G. (1996), Worship and Religious Education, *SPES,* **4**, May, 21–27.
Attfield, D. G. (1996), Learning from Religion, *British Journal of Religious Education*, **18. 2**, 78–84.
Badham, P. Ed. (1989), *Religion, State and Society in Modern Britain*, Edwin Mellen Press, Lampeter.
Baillie, D. (1948), *God Was In Christ,* Faber and Faber, London.
Ballard, P. H. Ed. (1986), *The Foundations of Pastoral Studies and Practical Theology,* Board of Pastoral Studies, University College, Cardiff.
Barbour, I. (1990), *Religion in an Age of Science*, S. C. M. Press, London.
Berger, P. L. (1973), *The Social Reality of Religion*, Penguin Books, London (1st Ed. Faber and Faber, 1969).
Black, P. (1985), *Mission: England*, Marc Europe, London.

Bowker, J. (1973), *The Sense of God: Sociological, Anthropological and Psychological Approaches to the Sense of God*, Oxford; (1978), *The Religious Imagination and the Sense of God*, Oxford.
Braine, D. (1988), *The Reality of Time and the Existence of God*, Clarendon Press, Oxford.
Brierley, P. (1991), *Christian England,* Marc Europe, London; (2000*)*, *The Tide is Running Out*, Christian Research, London.
Brooks, G., Gorman, T., Harman, T., Hutchinson, D., Wilkins, A. (1996), *Family Literacy Works*, Basic Skills Agency, London.
Browning, D. (1991), *A Fundamental Practical Theology,* Fortress Press, Minneapolis.
Bruce, F. (1995), *Religion in Modern Britain,* O. U. P., Oxford.
Bynner, J. and Steedman, J. (1995), *Difficulties with Basic Skills*, The Basic Skills Agency, London.
Camps, A. (1983), *Partners in Dialogue,* Orbis Books, Mary Knoll, N. Y.
Chadwick, O. (1990), *Michael Ramsey,* O. U. P., Oxford.
Christian Newsletter No 154 Supplement, 7th October 1942.
Clarke, J. (1995), *Evangelism that really works*, S. P. C. K., London.
Coakley, S. (1988), *Christ Without Absolutes,* Clarendon Press, Oxford.
Cottrell, S., Croft, S., Finney, J., Lawson, F. and Warren, R. (1996*)*, *Emmaus: The Way of Faith*, British and Foreign Bible Society, National Society, Church House Publishing, London/Swindon.
Cracknell, K. (1986), *Towards a New Relationship*, Epworth Press, London.
Cupitt, D. (1980), *Taking Leave of God,* S. C. M. Press, London; (1989), *Radicals and the Future of the Church*, S. C. M. Press, London.
D'Costa, G. (1986), *Theology and Religious Pluralism*, Blackwell, Oxford.
D.f.E. (1995), *The National Curriculum,* H. M. S. O., London.
Davie, G. (1994), *Religion in Britain since 1945*, Blackwell, Oxford.
Dearden, R. (1968), *The Philosophy of Primary Education,* Routledge and Kegan Paul, London.
Dearing, R. (1994), *The National Curriculum and its Assessment*, S. C. A. A., London.
Department for Education (D. f. E.) (1994), Circular 1/94, *Religious Education and Collective Worship,* London.
Dodd, C. H. (1935), *The Parables of the Kingdom*, Nisbet, London.
Downie, R. S. and Telfer, E. (1969), *Respect for Persons,* Allen and Unwin, London.
Duncan, B. (1991), *Church of England Clergy and Laity*, Manchester Cathedral 1991, (unpublished tables).
Educational Reform Act (1988)
Ekinsmyth, C. and Bynner J. (1994), *The Basic Skills of Young Adults*, The Basic Skills Agency, London
Farley, E. (1983), *Theologica: The Fragmentation and Unity of Theological Education,* Fortress Press, Philadelphia.

Festinger, L. (1957), *A Theory of Cognitive Dissonance*, Stanford University Press, California.
Finney, J. (1992), *Finding Faith Today*, British and Foreign Bible Society, Swindon.
Flew, A. G. N. and MacIntyre, A. C. (1955), *New Essays in Philosophical Theology*, S. C. M. Press, London.
Fowler, J. W. (1981), *Stages of Faith*, Harper Row, San Francisco.
Francis, L. J. (1996), Who wants RE? a socio–psychological profile of adolescent support for Religious Education, **14**, in Astley, J. and Francis L. J. Eds., *Christian Theology and Religious Education*, S. P. C. K., London.
Francis, L. J. and Wilcox C. (1996), Religion and Gender Orientation, *Person. individual. Differences*, **20**, 119–121; (1998), Religiosity and Femininity: Do Women really hold a more positive attitude to Christianity?, *Journal for the Scientific Study of Religion*, **37 (3)**, 462–469.
Freeman, A. (1993), *God in Us*, S. C. M. Press, London.
Gill, R. (1993), *The Myth of the Empty Church*, S. P. C. K., London.
Grant, W. H., Thompson, M., Clarke, T. E. (1983), *From Image to Likeness*, Paulist Press, Ramsey, New Jersey.
Groome, T. H. (1989), A Religious Education Response, in Browning, D. S., Polk, D. and Evison, I. S. Eds., *The Education of the Practical Theologian*, Scholars Press, Atlanta Georgia.
Gumbel, N. (1994), *Telling Others: the Alpha Initiative*, Kingsway Publications Ltd., Eastbourne.
Hardy, A. (1979), *The Spiritual Nature of Man*, Clarendon Press, Oxford.
Harvey, V. A. (1967), *The Historian and the Believer*, S. C. M. Press Ltd., London.
Haworth, L. (1986), *Autonomy*, Yale University Press, Newhaven and London.
Hay, D. (1990), *Religious Experience Today*, Mowbray, London.
Hebblethwaite, B. (1980), *The Problems of Theology*, C. U. P., Cambridge.
Hebblethwaite, B. (1984), *The Christian Hope*, Marshall, Morgan and Scott, Basingstoke.
Helm, P. (1997), *Faith and Understanding*, Edinburgh University Press, Edinburgh.
Hick, J. (1966), *Faith and Knowledge*, Macmillan, 2nd edition, London.
Hick, J., (1976), *Death and Eternal Life*, Collins, London.
Hick, J. (1989), *An Interpretation of Religion*, Macmillan, London.
Hirst, P. H. (1974), Liberal Education and the Nature of Knowledge in *Knowledge and the Curriculum*, Routledge and Kegan Paul, London.
Hobson, P. R. and Edwards, J. S. (1999), *Religious Education in a Pluralist Society*, Woburn Press, London.
Hodgson, L. *(1968), For Faith and Freedom*, S.C.M. Press, London, vol. I.
Hooker, M. D. (1991), *The Gospel according to St Mark*, A.C.Black, London.
Hooker, R. and Lamb C. (1986), *Love the Stranger*, S. P. C. K., London.
Hough, J. C. and Cobb, J. B. (1985), *Christian Identity and Christian Education*, Scholars Press, California.
Isaiah, Book of Prophet.

Jackson, R. (1997), *Religious Education: An Interpretative Approach,* Hodder and Stoughton, London.
Jeremias, J. (1954), *The Parables of Jesus,* S. C. M., London.
John St, Gospel of.
Jonathan, R. (1995), Education and Moral Development: the role of reason and circumstance, *Journal of the Philosophy of Education,* **29. 3,** Nov., 333–353.
Jung, C. (1921), *Psychological Types,* Princeton University Press, Princeton, New Jersey.
Kay, W. K. (1997), Belief in God in Britain 1945–1996, *British Journal of Religious Education,* **20. 1,** Autumn, 28–41.
Kay, W. K. and Francis, L. J. (1996),*Drift from the Churches,* University of Wales Press, Cardiff, **2.**
Kay, W. K., Francis, L. J. and Gibson H. M. (1996), Attitude to Christianity and the Transition to Formal Operational Thinking, *British Journal of Religious Education,* **19. 1,** Autumn, 36.
Keating, C. J. (1987), *Who We Are Is How We Pray,* 23A Publications Mystic, Connecticut.
Keirsey, P. and Bates, M. (1978), *Please Understand Me,* Prometheus Nemesis Book Co., Del Mar.
Kelly, J. N. D. *(1950), Early Christian Creeds,* Longmans, London.
Kelsey, D. H. (1992), *To Understand God Truly: What's Theological about a Theological School,* Westminster/John Knox Press, Louisville Kentucky.
Kohlberg, L. (1981), *Essays in Moral Development,* vol.1, Harper Row, London.
Kung, H. (1993), *Christianity and World Religions,* 2nd Ed. S. C. M. Press, London.
Levinson, M. (1999), *the demands of liberal education,* O. U. P., Oxford 1999.
Lewis, H. D. (1959), *Our Experience of God,* Allen and Unwin, London.
Lonergan, B. (1958), *Insight,* Harper Row, New York; (1972) *Method in Theology,* Darton, Longman and Todd, London.
Loukes, H. (1965), *New Ground in Christian Education ,* S. C. M. Press, London.
Luke, St Gospel of.
Luntley, M. (2000), *Performance, Pay and Professionals,* Philosophy of Education Society of Great Britain, London.
Mackinnon, D., (1972), Theology as a Discipline of a Modern University, in Shanin, T. Ed., *The Rules of the Game,* Tavistock Publications, London, 164–175.
Mark, St Gospel of.
Markham, I. (1998), *Truth and the Reality of God,* T. and T. Clark, Edinburgh.
Matthew, St Gospel of.
McIntyre, A. (1988), *Whose Justice? Which Rationality?,* Duckworth, London and Notre Dame University Press, Notre Dame.
Mitchell, B. (1994), *Faith and Criticism,* Clarendon Press, Oxford; (1973), *The Justification of Religious Belief,* Macmillan, London.

Montefiore, H. (1985), *The Probability of God*, S. C. M. Press, London; (1992), *The Gospel and Contemporary Culture,* Mowbray, London.
Morris, T. V. Ed. (1994), *God and the Philosopher,* New York/ Oxford University Press.
National Curriculum Council (1990), *The Whole Curriculum*, Curriculum Guidance No.3., York.
National Society (1992), *All God's Children,*(G. S. 988), London.
Newbigin, L. (1983),*The Other Side of 84*, W. C. C. Geneva; (1986), *Foolishness to the* Greeks, S. P. C. K.; (1989), *The Gospel in a Pluralist Society*, S. P. C. K. London; (1991), *Truth to Tell*, S. P. C. K., London.
Norman, R. (1994),"I did it my way." Some Thoughts on Autonomy, *Journal of the Philosophy of Education*, **28. 1,** 25–34.
OFSTED, *Primary Education: Review of Primary Schools in England 1994–98*, **3. 1**, Chart 12 and 13.
Oman, J. (1925), *Grace and Personality*, Cambridge, 3rd Ed.
Pascal, B. (1950), *Pensées*, (E. T.) H.F.Stewart, Routledge and Kegan Paul, London.
Payne Best, (1953), The Venlo Incident, in Bethge, E. Ed., *Dietrich Bonhoeffer, Letters and Papers from Prison*, (E.T.) Fuller R. H., S. C. M. Press, London, 11.
Peters, R. S. (1996), *Ethics and Education*, Allen and Unwin, London; (1967), *The Concept of Education*, Routledge, London; (1973), *Reason and Compassion*, Routledge and Kegan Paul, London.
Peters, R. S. (1972), Reason and Passion, in Dearden, R. F., Hirst, P. H. and Peters, R. S. Eds., *Education and the Development of Reason,* Routledge and Kegan Paul, London, **12**.
Philippians, Epistle to.
Plantinga, A. and Wolterstorff, N. Eds. (1983), *Faith and Rationality,* University of Notre Dame Press, London.
Price, H. H. (1964), Faith and Belief in Hick, J. Ed., *Faith and the Philosophers*, Macmillan, London, 3–25.
Qualifications and Curriculum Authority (2000), *Religious Education: non-statutory guidance, Q*.C.A./00/576, London.
Quality Assurance Agency for Higher Education in the UK, *Teaching Quality Assessments.*
Qur'an
Reeves, M. Ed. (1999), *Christian Thinking and Social Order*, Cassell, London.
Riesman, D., (1950) *The Lonely Crowd,* Yale University Press, Newhaven; *Individualism Reconsidered* (1954), Free Press of Glencoe, New York 1954.
Runzo, J. Ed. (1993), *Is God Real?* Macmillan, London
Schon, D.A. (1983), *The Reflective Practitioner,* Harper Collins, USA.
Schools Curriculum and Assessment Authority (1994), *Model Syllabuses for Religious Education Consultation Document,* Introduction.
Schwarz, C. (1996), *Natural Church Development*, (UK Ed.), British Church Growth Association, Moggerhanger.

Sider, R. (1993), *Evangelism and Social Action*, Hodder and Stoughton, London.
Smart, J. J. C. and Haldane J. J. (1996), *Atheism and Theism*, Blackwell, Oxford.
Smart, N. (1960), *A Dialogue of Religions*, S. C. M. Press, London; (1973), *The Phenomenon of Religion*, Macmillan, London; (1981), *Beyond Ideology*, Collins, London.
Smart, N. (1989), **20**, *Church, Party and State* in Badham, op cit.
Snook, I. A. (1972), *Indoctrination and Education*, Routledge and Kegan Paul; London; and *Concepts of Indoctrination* Ed., Routledge and Kegan Paul, London.
Spriggs, D. (1995), *Transition Times*, Church Growth Digest **16. 3**, Spring, 3–4.
Swinburne, R., (1970), *The Concept of Miracles*, Macmillan, London; (1979), *The Existence of God*, Clarendon Press, Oxford; (1992), *Revelation*, Clarendon Press, Oxford; (1997), *The Coherence of Theism*, Clarendon Press, Oxford.
Thiessen, E. J. (1993), *Teaching for Commitment*, Gracewing Leominster.
Tillich, P. (1947), *The Shaking of the Foundation*, S. C. M. Press, London.
Weil, S. (1950), *Waiting on God*, Collins Fontana, (E. T.), Crawford, London.
White, J. (1967), *Indoctrination* **11**, 177–191 in Peters (1967), op. cit.
Wooderson, M. (1982), *No.9 Grove Books*, Bramcote, Notts.
Yarnold, E. (1974), *The Second Gift*, St. Paul's Publications, Slough.

Index

academic study of religion 7–8, 9, 17, 38, 50, 75
  application of theory of religious communication 105–7
  autonomy and 108, 141
  commitment and 107–8, 143
  exploration and 109, 143
  learning and 109, 142–3
  motivation 108–9, 142
  nourishing the sense of God and 142
  opportunity 108, 141–2
  remediation 125
  theology 107–8, 112–14
  training the communicators 141–3
  verbal ability and 141
accommodation 83–4
after-life 154–5
age
  literacy and 38
  opportunities for learning and exploration and 43
  religious communication and 20
Alpha Courses 97, 129, 131
Amnesty International 65
applied theology 114
atonement 81
Attfield, David G., autobiographical details 1–2
autonomy 19–20
  academic study of religion and 108, 141
  development of autonomy in children 41–2
  education and 20, 24, 40, 42
  evangelism and 97–8, 129
  gender and 41
  inter-faith dialogue and 100–101, 132
  ministerial formation and 110, 144
  nurture and 102, 134
  religious communication and 32, 40–42, 97–8
  religious education and 139
  remediation 123
  resources and 121
  training the communicators 129, 132

baptism 91
Barbour, I. 78, 79
belief-systems 74, 76, 86
Bible
  creation in 80, 82
  parable of the sower 150–54
  study of 112
  truth criteria and 81–2
Bonhoeffer, Dietrich 52
British Council of Churches, guidelines for inter-faith dialogue 99–100
Buddhism 85, 92, 132

Calvin, Jean 85, 88, 90
campaigns 19–20
Catherine of Genoa 88
children
  development of autonomy 41–2
  evangelism and 5, 6
  nurture 6–7, 18–19
    application of theory of religious communication 104–5
    commitment and 138
    exploration and 137–8
    failure of 16
    learning and 75–6, 136–7
    motivation 136
    nourishing the sense of God 136
    opportunity and 136

remediation 124
training the communicators
  135–8
verbal ability and 104, 135–6
see also education
choice
  religion and 11, 32, 91
  see also commitment
Christian Frontier Council 65
Christianity
  beliefs 49, 74, 83
  committed and non-committed 4
  communication of *see* religious
    communication
  definition of Christian 3
  message of 11, 12
  morality and 74
  practising and non-practising 3–4,
    50
  social context 10
Church of England
  author's experience of 1–2
  new contacts with 18
Churches Together 3
Finding Faith Today 17–18
class 69
  literacy and 38
  motivation and 70
  religious communication and 20
cognitive dissonance 28–9, 61–2,
  64–5, 66, 67
commitment 4, 9
  academic study of religion and
    107–8, 143
  evangelism and 5, 131
  inter-faith dialogue and 91–2,
    102, 134
  ministerial formation and 8, 92–3,
    146
  nurture of 6–7, 8, 92, 135
    children 138
  religious education and 92, 93,
    141
  stage of religious communication
    model 27, 28, 31, 90–93

training the communicators 131
communication, religious *see*
  religious communication
communicators 127–8
  model for 33–4
  training *see* training the
    communicators
confirmation 4, 91, 138
congregations, quality of 22–3
contingency, reflection and
  nourishing the sense of God and
  52–3
conversion 5–6, 18, 102
creation 56–7, 80, 82, 84
credulity, principle of 57–8, 89
Creeds 74
critical realism 56
crusade evangelism 19–20
curiosity 30, 51

damnation 81
determinism 80
drama 65

education
  autonomy and 20, 24, 40, 42
  literacy and 37–8, 39–40
  opportunities for learning and
    exploration 33, 43–4
  religious *see* religious education
Education Reform Act 1988 10
Edwards, J. S. 78
Emmaus Courses 97, 129
emotional aspect of faith 74–5
empowerment of leadership 23
enthusiasm 19, 23
epistemology, reformed 85–90
Erikson, 2
Eucharist 74
evangelism
  in after-life 154–5
  application of theory of religious
    communication 97–9
  autonomy and 97–8, 129
  children and 5, 6

commitment and 5, 131
conversion and 5–6, 102
crusade evangelism 19–20
definition of 5
exploration and 131
failure of 16
learning and 75, 131
motivation and 98, 130–31
need-oriented 23
nourishing the sense of God and 97, 98, 130
opportunity and 98–9, 129–30
training the communicators 128–31
verbal ability and 97, 128–9
evil 81, 87
evolution 80, 82
experience, reality/existence of God and religious experience 57–8, 82–3, 89–90
exploration
  academic study of religion and 109, 143
  evangelism and 131
  inter-faith dialogue and 75, 101–2, 133–4
  ministerial formation and 111–12, 146
  nurture and 103–4, 135
    children 137–8
  opportunities for 33, 43–4
  religious education and 105–6, 140–41
  stage of religious communication model 27, 28, 31, 76–9
  training the communicators 131

falsification controversies 78
Finding Faith Today (Churches Together) 17–18
foundationalism 86
Fowler, James 2, 3, 31, 40
Francis of Assisi, Saint 88
Francis, Leslie 21, 38
Free Churches, new contacts with 18

free will 80
Freudianism 57, 87
friendship 66–7, 133

Gandhi, Mahatma 88
gender 69
  autonomy and 41
  literacy and 38–9
  motivation and 69–70
  religious communication and 20, 21–2, 38–9, 69–70, 129
God 79
  creation and 56–7, 80, 82, 84
  grace 118–20
  inter-religious truth criteria and 83–5
  reality/existence of 47, 55–9, 74, 86, 87, 88
    religious experience and 57–8, 82–3, 89–90
  sense of 47–9
    assessment of 54–5
    nourishing *see* nourishing the sense of God
  theism 30, 47–8, 54, 55, 78, 86, 87
  theology 107–8, 112–14
  Trinity 80, 84
Gospel and Culture Movement 65
Gospel/Good News Down the Street 68, 97, 130
grace, human effort and 118–20
Graham, Billy 19–20, 21
groups, holistic small groups 23–4
guilt 39
  original 81

al-Hallaj 88
hermeneutics 114
Hick, J. 88
Hinduism 92
  concept of deity in 49, 83, 84, 85
history 65–6, 81, 83
Hobson, P. R. 78
holistic small groups 23–4

hospital chaplaincy 113
Hume, David 86
idiosyncratic commitment 91
incorrigibility 86
indoctrination 11
inductive reasoning 114
inter-faith dialogue 5–6, 17, 38, 50
    application of theory of religious communication 99–102
    autonomy and 100–101, 132
    British Council of Churches guidelines 99–100
    commitment and 91–2, 102, 134
    exploration and 75, 101–2, 133–4
    learning and 75, 101, 133
    motivation and 101, 133
    nourishing the sense of God and 132–3
    opportunity for 101, 132
    training the communicators 132–4
    verbal ability and 100, 132
inter-religious truth criteria 83–5
interest
    generation of 28–30
    see also nourishing the sense of God
intra-religious truth criteria 81–3
Islam 91
    concept of deity in 49, 83, 84

Jesus Christ 79, 80, 81, 88, 137
    parable of the sower 150–54
Judaism, concept of deity in 49, 83
Julian of Norwich 88
Jung, Carl 62

Kant, Immanuel 112
King, Martin Luther 88
Kohlberg, L. 2, 31
Koran/Qur'an 84, 91

lay ministry 23
leadership
    empowerment of 23
    see also ministry

learning
    academic study of religion and 109, 142–3
    evangelism and 75, 131
    inter-faith dialogue and 75, 101, 133
    ministerial formation and 111, 145–6
    nurture and 75, 135
        children 136–7
    opportunities for 33, 43–4
    religious education and 75, 140
    stage of religious communication model 27, 31, 73–6
    training the communicators 131
literacy 32, 37–40
Locke, John 86
logic 80, 86

Markham, I. 56
marriage 91
Marxism 57, 87
meditation, nourishing the sense of God and 52–3
membership of churches 138
    decline in 15–17
    definition of Christian and 3
memory 87
ministerial formation 17, 38, 50, 75
    application of theory of religious communication 109–15
    autonomy and 110, 144
    commitment and 8, 92–3, 146
    exploration and 111–12, 146
    learning and 111, 145–6
    motivation 145
    nourishing the sense of God and 145
    nurture and 8, 92–3
    opportunity 110–11, 144
    remediation 126
    training the communicators 144–6
    verbal ability and 144
ministry
    autobiographical details 1–2

lay 23
training for *see* ministerial formation
miracles 81
Mission England 19–20
morality 74, 81, 83
Moses 79, 88
motivation 11, 25, 102–3
  academic study of religion 108–9, 142
  child nurture and 136
  class and 70
  evangelism and 98, 130–31
  gender and 69–70
  inter-faith dialogue and 101, 133
  ministerial formation and 145
  Myers-Briggs typology and 61–7
  other categorisations and 69–70
  religious education and 68, 106–7, 140
  resources for 122
  stage of religious communication model 27–8, 30, 61–70, 98
  training the communicators 130–31
Muhammad 79, 88, 91
Myers, Isobel Briggs 62
Myers-Briggs typology
  communication and 67–9
  motivation and 61–7, 98, 131
mystics 11

Nanak, Guru 88
Natural Church Development strategy 22–4
need-oriented evangelism 23
Newbigin, L. 54, 100
non-realist versions of religion 11
nourishing the sense of God 30–31, 47–59, 97, 103
  academic study of religion and 142
  evangelism and 97, 98, 130
  inter-faith dialogue and 132–3
  ministerial formation and 145

nurture 134–5
  children 136
  reflection/meditation and 52–3
  religious education and 49–51, 59, 98, 139–40
  remediation 124
  resources for 121–2
  training the communicators 130
  witness and 51–2
  worship and 49, 50–51, 139
nurture 6
  application of theory of religious communication 102–4
  autonomy and 102, 134
  children 6–7, 18–19
    application of theory of religious communication 104–5
    commitment and 138
    exploration and 137–8
    failure of 16
    learning and 75–6, 136–7
    motivation 136
    nourishing the sense of God 136
    opportunity and 136
    remediation 124
    training the communicators 135–8
    verbal ability and 104, 135–6
  commitment and 6–7, 8, 92, 135
  exploration and 103–4, 135
    children 137–8
  failure of 16–17
  learning and 75, 135
    children 136–7
  ministerial formation and 8, 92–3
  nourishing the sense of God 134–5
  opportunity for 103
  training the communicators 134–5

objectivity 56, 76, 77, 86
opportunity stage in religious communication 33, 43–4

academic study of religion and 108, 141–2
  evangelism and 98–9, 129–30
  inter-faith dialogue and 101, 132
  ministerial formation and 110–11, 144
  nurture and 103
    children 136
  religious education and 106, 139
  training the communicators 129–30
oracy 37, 39, 40
over-expansion thesis 16
Oxfam 65

parable of the sower 150–54
Pascal, Blaise 77
passionate spirituality 23
Paul, Saint 88, 119
penal substitutionary theory 81
perfected steps fallacy 31
perspectivism 56
philosophy 86
  philosophical argument 84–5
Piaget, J. 2
Plantinga, Alvin 85
pluralism 10
prayer 74, 80, 113
pre-religious truth criteria 80–81
priesthood *see* ministry
privacy, religion as private affair 29
propaganda 11
prophets 66, 79, 82
providence 80

quality of congregations 22–3
Qur'an 84, 91

Ramanuja 88
Ramsay, Michael 52
realist versions of religion 11
reflection, nourishing the sense of God and 52–3
reformed epistemology 85–90
relationships

friendship 66–7, 133
  within churches 23
relativism 56, 78
religious communication
  autobiographical details 1–2
  normal process of 17–19
  parable of the sower and 150–54
  problems 15–22, 123–6
  requirements of 24–5
  special process of 19–20
  theory of 2, 27–34, 149–56
    adding fifth stage 28–31
    application 97–115
    assumptions 9–12
    background conditions 31–3, 37–44
    Communicator's model 33–4
    definition of key terms 2–4
    four-stage model 27–8
    objections 117–26
    species of communication 4–9
    summary 149–50
  training in *see* training the communicators
  see also individual topics
religious education 1, 7, 9, 10, 19, 30
  application of theory of religious communication 104–7
  autonomy and 139
  commitment and 92, 93, 141
  exploration and 105–6, 140–41
  failure of 17
  learning and 75, 140
  motivation and 68, 106–7, 140
  nourishing the sense of God and 49–51, 59, 98, 139–40
  opportunity 106, 139
  remediation 124–5
  training the communicators 136–7, 138–41
  verbal ability and 106, 138–9
  see also academic study of religion
religious experience,
  reality/existence of God and 57–8,

82–3, 89–90
remediation 123–6
resources, lack of 120–22
Riesman, David 40
Roman Catholic church, new
   contacts with 18

Schwarz, C. 22
science 56, 78, 113
secularity of modern society 10, 16,
   29–30, 54, 87
self-direction *see* autonomy
self-evidence 86
self-interest 28, 30
sex *see* gender
Shelter 65
Sikhism, concept of deity in 49, 83
sin 74
social action 29–30
social class *see* class
social context 10
social gospel 117–18, 121
social sciences 113
spirituality, passion and 23
stage theories 2
   theory of religious communication
      adding fifth stage 28–31
      four-stage model 27–8
structures, functional 23
subjective interpretation of religion
   76
Swinburne, R. 56, 57, 89

syncretism 91

theism 30, 47–8, 54, 55, 78, 86, 87
theology 107–8, 112–14
Theresa, Mother 88
Thomas, Saint 138
training the communicators 127–47
   academic study of religion 141–3
   evangelism 128–31
   inter-faith dialogue 132–4
   ministerial formation 144–6
   nurture of adults 134–5
   nurture of children 135–8
   religious education 138–41
   who are the communicators 127–8

Weil, Simone 3
Wilcox, Carolyn 21, 38
witness, nourishing the sense of God
   and 51–2, 98
Wolterstorff, Nicholas 86
World Council of Churches 3
worship
   inspiring worship service 23
   learning about 74
   nourishing the sense of God and
      49, 50–51, 139
   nurture and 102–3
      nourishing the sense of God
         and 49, 50–51